What Not to Expect

What Not to Expect

A Meditation on the Spirituality of Parenting

KEITH W. FROME

A Crossroad Book
Crossroad Publishing Company
New York

The Crossroad Publishing Company
www.CrossroadPublishing.com

Printed in the United States of America

This book is set in 11/14 AGaramond.
The display type is Sanvito Roman.

Library of Congress Cataloging-in-Publication Data

Frome, Keith.
    What not to expect : a meditation on the spirituality of parenting /
Keith W. Frome.
        p. cm.
    Includes bibliographical references (p.   ) and index.
    ISBN 0-8245-2282-6 (alk. paper)
    1. Parenting—Religious aspects. I. Title.
BL625.8.F76 2005
204'.41—dc22
                                                2005005516

To
Henry
Spencer
Ermelinda

~

Thank you John for believing in me, then and now

Gee, Dad, I guess there's a lot more to being a father than making money and hollering.

—The Beaver

~

I prefer not to speculate. That's the daily task, in my view. A refusal to speculate, only encounter. Only understand.

—Abraham Ebdus in Jonathan Lethem,
The Fortress of Solitude

~

Apart from the daily experience, there is no religious life, so Satori is an occurrence of daily life, with its joys and sorrows.

—Reverend Kaneko

~

Paradise is hidden in each one of us, it is concealed within me, too, right now, and if I wish, it will come for me, in reality, tomorrow even, and for the rest of my life . . .

—The Mysterious Stranger in Dostoevsky,
The Brothers Karamazov

~

When a dog loves her master, it's just all-out love. She doesn't hold anything back. She won't stop licking you until you literally push her away. She never can get enough of your petting. A dog has no distance between her love and her behavior. No amount of love is too much, either to give or to receive. That's why a dog needs discipline, so she doesn't make an idiot of herself. These thoughts never occurred to me when Tiffany was alive, but since her death I've become more human, in a way. Always there's that space between what you feel and what you do, and in that gap all human sadness lies.

—George Rodrigue and Lawrence S. Freundlich,
Blue Dog

~

Alas for those who counsel sternness and severity instead of love towards their young children! How little they are like God, how much they are like Solomon, whom I really believe many persons prefer to imitate, and think they do well. Infinite patience, infinite tenderness, infinite magnanimity—no less will do, and we must practise them as far as finite power will allow. Above all, no parent should feel a pride of power. This, I doubt not, is the great stumbling-block, and it should never be indulged.

—Sophia Hawthorne

~

FOUR-YEAR-OLD: Daddy, I'm scared.
DAD: How can you be scared? Your Daddy's with you.
FOUR-YEAR-OLD'S SEVEN-YEAR-OLD BROTHER: Maybe Dads can't protect you from everything.
DAD: Thanks.
FOUR-YEAR-OLD'S SEVEN-YEAR-OLD BROTHER: I'm just trying to tell him the score.

Contents

	A Note on Bias and Privacy	xi
1	You Can't Always Get What You Want	1
2	Knowing	18
3	Disappointing	25
4	Playing	32
5	Pooping	39
6	Emotions	47
7	Toys and Possessions	55
8	Discipline	63
9	Doubling: On They Being You	72
10	Rituals	81
11	Gossip	90
12	Interests	100
13	Questions	111
14	Schooling	122
15	Injuries, Falls, Sickness, and Failure	133
16	Love and Community	144
	Works Cited	153
	Index	157

A Note on Bias and Privacy

I WROTE THIS BOOK OUT OF MY EXPERIENCES AS A father and as a headmaster. I have young children, so many of the stories concern early childhood rather than adolescence or adult children. I live in Buffalo; hence you will hear more about hockey as opposed to, say, basketball or surfing. I run an independent school, hence my thoughts on schooling will not be informed by the public system. I'm male. I write from the vantage point of a professional U.S. citizen at the turn of the century. My wife and I live together. I have two sons. I could go on and on, but to list all of my biases would be to write my tedious autobiography. Everyone writes and speaks and lives according to a set of biases. These assumptions form the platform for our ideas, our stories, and our judgments. We cannot help this; we are limited. I hope that all parents, no matter their gender or sexual orientation or economic status or family structure, can enjoy and get something out of this book. Nevertheless, I know that not all families are alike (even happy ones) and that people parent in many different ways. In a way, this is the very thesis of this book. It is an anti-advice book. Still, parents are, in all of our differences, bound together as seekers in the grasp of a profound mystery. We tend to all face the same challenges. If we stopped and looked and listened to our children, if we meditated on the moments of parenting, what would we find? One question can yield a multitude of answers.

All of the anecdotes in this book are true in their essence and message. Sometimes I have changed names, genders, or locations to maintain confidentiality. Any similarity between the names and stories described in this book and those people known to my readers, except for tales from my own immediate family, are purely coincidental.

1

You Can't Always Get What You Want

WHEN MY YOUNGEST SON, SPENCER, WAS TWO, HIS FAVORITE song was "You Can't Always Get What You Want" by the Rolling Stones. Just barely beginning to talk, he would make me play the song over and over again, singing "Can't aways ge wha you wanna but if you try time you get need." I loved his faulty articulation, especially the notion of trying time, as though time was something you could sample and then discard if you found it unsatisfying.

In any case, my wife and I were concerned. The other toddlers were singing Barney songs, and we feared that Spencer's teachers would think us irresponsible for introducing our little boy to Keith Richard and Mick Jagger's sordid world of drug-addicted artsy models. But Spencer never asked or cared why the narrator of the song had to go to the Chelsea Drug Store. He was only interested in singing the chorus.

We eventually decided that this song expressed the perfect sentiment for a two-year-old growing up in a comfortable American home. Our house is full of toys and games and balls and bats and hockey sticks. I couldn't help thinking that as Spencer smiled at me and sang along with Mick, he was telling me, however unconsciously, that I had a spiritual duty to teach him what he needed deep down. He was reminding us that his needs went beyond soothing ointments, good food, and toys.

At the time, I was teaching an introductory undergraduate class in world religions, and it seemed to me that the chorus's refrain summed up the wisdom of all of the religions my students were studying. This in turn led me to reflect on how parents can turn to certain philosophers and the wisdom of the world's faith traditions to guide them through their journey as caregivers. My purpose in this book is not to help parents teach their children about the world's religions, though that is a wonderful thing to do with your child. To the already well-stocked bookshelf of parent help books, I want to add an advice book that gives no advice. Picture your local bookstore. Go to the parenting section. You will see a long line of book spines glazed in primary colors written by experts in medicine, developmental psychology, education, and the social sciences. But in all of the variety of parenting books, you will rarely find the wisdom of the Hebrew Bible, the New Testament, the *Bhagavad-Gita*, the Qur'an, the *Lotus Sutra*, or the *Tao Tê Ching*. There is very little mysticism in the parent advice library. The closest I've come to this is at my local Barnes & Noble in Amherst, New York, where World Religions titles are directly behind Parenting and Education. To satisfy my twin interests, I only need to pivot back and forth as I browse the stacks.

Which is exactly what I plan to do in the following chapters.

My wife and I and millions of other parents have hungrily consulted the series *What to Expect* by Arlene Eisenberg, Heidi E. Murkoff, and Sandee E. Hathaway. Each book details the month-by-month problems, challenges, and developmental goals of the fetus, the one-year-old, the toddler, and so on. The cheery and confident trio of nurses dispense excellent advice about nutrition and colds and temper tantrums and car seats. Beyond the advice, the book gives us parents ways to track the developmental growth of our baby and toddler. The checklist for each month of growth has four levels: what your child should be doing; will probably be able to do; may possibly be able to do; and may even be able to do.

I will admit it—my wife and I graded our sons on these milestones each month. How could we help ourselves? We had lived and thrived by the grading system our whole lives. Here was another report card to master. We wanted to know just what kind of boys we had produced. Was Henry, at two months, a "may possibly be able to do" child or was he, fingers crossed, a boy in the "may even be able to do" category?

We had the proper dose of irony and guilt about stuffing our baby into one of the four pigeonholes. We even created a fifth category: "May even possibly beyond your wildest Ivy League expectations and parental fantasies be able to do." Still, to be honest, we took the developmental checklist seriously and filled it out each month, if only to be reassured—because we really didn't know what to expect. The *What to Expect* books are therapeutic because they create a set of common experiences and a benevolent priesthood of knowers who assure us that they have been there before.

This metaphor of expectation pervades all of the books in the parenting section, for it calms the panicked, ignorant mom and dad. You can't believe that this living being came out of the mere mixing of bodily fluids, and as magically as your baby appeared, you think, she can just as easily disappear. The unexpected is the primal fear of all parents.

It is also the same state of awe experienced by spiritual people around the world. Parenting books accept this fact and then deny it, saying, in effect, what you find unexpected (two hours of sleep a night, unmitigated crying) is actually expected. I have a friend, a fellow parent, who, when talking about the challenges of raising a family, constantly says, "Well you know what *they* say. . . ." I always wonder who the "they" are? Do they live on her street?

Why are they always telling my friend what to do? "They" are the advisors in parenting books and magazines who reduce problems to their simplest structures and then give solutions. These priests of parenting demystify, in contrast to the wise priests and rabbis and monks and mullahs and yogis of the world's religions who celebrate and intensify the mystery.

This is the difference between religion and the social and medical sciences. What if we turned the parenting advice industry on its head and consulted advisors who would urge us to embrace the questions and to avoid easy, reductive answers? I have kept an old T-shirt from the Religious Studies Department at Wellesley College that asks on the front "Why study religion?" and answers on the back "Magic, Mystery, Madness." As a graduate student, I wore the T-shirt as a banner announcing my major field of study. I now wear it to share with passersby what it's like to be a parent.

∿

The twenty-first-century parent
sees disaster looming around every corner.

∿

I became the headmaster of an independent school at exactly the same time I became a father. For the last seven years, parenting and raising and educating children have been the constant anxieties of my public days and my private nights. Peter Stearns, in his book *Anxious Parents: A History of Modern Childrearing in America*, argues that parents are now more anxious than ever because they believe that their children are vulnerable beings whose physical and mental health is everywhere threatened. In the early decades of the twentieth century, parents enjoyed a more confident and optimistic paradigm of childhood, according to

Stearns. They assumed that children were essentially strong and sturdy. As the century progressed, Stearns explains that psychologists, educational theorists, and the omnipresent media led parents to believe that their children were actually fragile beings in danger everywhere.

While I cannot verify Stearns's historical research, I can say as a parent and headmaster that he's absolutely correct to identify anxiety as the major attribute of today's American parents—at least the ones that I know as friends and clients. I observe many parents who try to manage every aspect of their children's lives. They seek to control each variable of their kids' experiences lest one event turn out to be the cause leading to their eventual unraveling. Like the classic pushy parents of a child actor, many parents seek to be the agent of their child's success. And, as in show business, they see the business of life as exceedingly fragile. Your child may be the best reader in first grade, but you never know about next year, unless you play your cards right and hire the most gifted and charismatic tutor.

The twenty-first-century parent sees disaster looming around every corner. It could be a failed spelling test in the second grade that breaks Bobby's love of language. It could be the wrong role in the school play that will destroy Jane's desire to pursue a Broadway career. Once a parent complained to me that his son was cast as a rooster in the school adaptation of *True Grit*. He believed that casting his boy as an animal would crush the budding thespian's theatrical self-esteem. When we explained that his son was not going to play a fowl but was actually chosen to play a character named Rooster, the starring role in the production, the father remained unsatisfied, because he thought it clumsy to have to explain this distinction to his friends and colleagues.

Some parents blame teachers for their child's low grades, claiming that if they had received enough advanced warning they could have rescued their son or daughter from a D or an F by hiring a tutor or teaching the subject themselves. Parents these days try, in so many different ways, to become rescue heroes. Being a parental rescue hero is exhausting work. To be a competent one, you must seek to control and perfect your child's environment. You must have near complete knowledge of pediatrics, education, and psychology. You must be an expert in athletics, sociology, environmental science, college admissions, the media, time management, nutrition, hygiene, genetics, learning styles, pedagogy, allergies, conflict resolution, semantics, the toy industry, and technology. You must also understand the depth and breadth of all of the subjects of the school's curriculum.

Perfect knowledge is not enough, though, for the parent rescue hero. Moms and dads must also be masters of communication, administration, and personnel evaluation. Parent rescue heroes need to set goals for their children, create and find structures within which their children can achieve these goals, and employ evaluation tools to monitor performance and success. Since they can't humanly do everything, parent rescue heroes must hire a team of highly qualified, but usually poorly compensated, professionals to work with their children. These employees—teachers, pediatricians, nannies, and coaches—are recruited, evaluated, assessed, and, if necessary, fired (or downsized, as the case may be). Raising children has become a major service industry. Each child is a product and their parents are the CEOs.

Just what do we want these products to look like? I think parents don't desire anything different from parents from earlier eras. They want safe, healthy, happy children who have every opportunity to fulfill their potential. What's different is that contemporary parents fear that their children may never recover if they ever fail or get injured or are disappointed. The threat of terrorism is not only our daily reality but our nation's dominant parenting metaphor. In the same way that we are ever vigilant for the sniper or the bomb or the hijacked plane that will come out of nowhere and destroy our lives, parents feel that they must guard every aspect of their child's existence lest she suffer a blow to her sense of self that will hobble her forever.

Beneath this umbrella of anxiety, all parents share one thing with caretakers from other generations: each day they confront the ordinary. By the ordinary, I mean the daily, cyclical tasks and mundane demands of taking care of children—from cooking dinner to drawing a bath to playing superheroes in the backyard to driving to play dates to reading bedtime stories. No matter your profession, no matter your level of education, no matter how much poetry in your soul, parenting is essentially a matter of tending to the basic, earthy needs of your children. It is a necklace of chores.

I once met with a wealthy, glamorous, and exquisitely dignified philanthropist. She lived in an elegant mansion full of art and antiques. We were speaking of raising money when she asked if she could change the subject, noting that we both had six-year-old boys. She wanted to know if my son still wanted me to wipe him after he went to the bathroom. She still had to administer to her son, and she wanted to know if this was normal. No matter your lot in life, parenting comes down to these kinds of questions and concerns.

Parenting brings us back to the base, physical facts of being human. It is intensely primal. We worry about digestion and sleep. Becoming a parent releases us from us the abstract clouds of our young adulthood and slams us back to earth into the muck of being alive. In my experience, I have witnessed four basic ways that parents confront the primacy of the ordinary.

1. The **dutiful parent** sees the ordinary rounds of parenting to be the chores every parent ought to perform to raise healthy children. In this way of viewing the ordinary, parents are administrators whose job it is to provide all that is necessary for the care and feeding of their young ones.

2. The **narcissistic parent** sees himself reflected in every aspect of his children's lives. This kind of parent continually refers back to his experiences as a child. The narcissistic parent either wants to recreate the conditions of his upbringing because he idolizes his own parents or he wants to upend his upbringing because he demonizes his parents. In either case, children of narcissistic parents are not seen as individuals but as characters in the psychodrama of their parent; the ordinary chores of parenting become reenactments of the sentimental or the horrific scenes in this drama.

3. The **aesthetic parent** sees the extraordinary in the ordinary rounds of parenting. Like an artist, the aesthetic parent sees beauty in diapers, in mixing and mashing pears and apples for baby food, in the pattern of the spill of tomato sauce on the father's apron, in the tantrums of their toddlers. This kind of parent romanticizes childhood. Their house is adorned with photos of the silhouettes of children running naked on a beach at sunset. Aesthetic parents are romantic poets who believe that infants are wise and that children should be the teachers of adults. Usually, the aesthetic parent becomes demoralized as their children grow older, exhibit complexity, and reveal the ugly parts of the family's soul.

4. The **religious parent** sees parenting as a mystery. Religious parents primarily feel awe, respect, and reverence. They do not worship their child, as the narcissistic or aesthetic parent might. But they do worship, in a sense, the miracle of the cycle of life and are humbled by it. Mirroring the techniques of Zen meditation, the religious parent fully focuses on the moments of parenting. They are right there, tending to their child as a fully realized other. Their children are not abstractions or projections of their own fantasies and anxieties. By "religious" I do not mean any kind of institutional religion. I mean a spiritual feeling of connection to some-

thing beyond ourselves and beyond our understanding. The book reviewer Louis Bayard said recently, "Religion is at heart a closed system—a ring of certainty." I think he gets this just exactly wrong. The religious impulse is to embrace uncertainty and to position one's self inside the circle of something we can never hope to understand intellectually. The end of spirituality and the religious institutions that hope to foster a community of religious seekers is indeed this "Peace that passeth all understanding."

Dutiful, narcissistic, and aesthetic parents share a common trait. They all view the value of the child through the lens of an external criterion. This benchmark may be their own lives, a notion of beauty, or ideas about what is "best." The religious or spiritual parent incorporates the best practices of all the various parenting styles and philosophies. The difference is that spiritual parents behold their child as she eats, sleeps, plays, misbehaves, fails, and succeeds from a reverential mind-set of awe and wonder. Their work as parents flows directly from a core understanding that they are part of something much larger than themselves. Hence, spiritual parents combine humility and confidence. Parents and children walk together as free and distinct individuals against an infinite horizon that frames their every movement and at the same time liberates them to constantly grow and to become.

(In addition to these four types of parenting, there are also neglectful and abusive parents who create living hells for their children. In this type of parenting, which is tragically too common, the world of the ordinary becomes extraordinary. An abused child's existence is characterized, among other things, by the absence of normal, ordinary routines of life. Eating, sleeping, and playing become dangerous opportunities in an abusive household. I don't think that you can count this as a fifth mode of parenting since it is so pathological.)

The modern, anxious parent is fearful precisely because she is ever vigilant to avoid any kind of potentially abusive environment for her children. She sees the potential for abuse in every setting, even in her own living room. There is another, more unconscious factor that contributes to the stress of the modern parent. We, without realizing it, automatically embrace mechanistic ways of knowing. In most of Western society, to know something as true is to be able to reduce it to the predictability of a machine. Knowledge is defined as the ability to organize, to categorize, to systematize, and to make a complex phenomenon like parenting simple so that we may control the present and predict the future. Parents think that good parenting is really a matter of following a recipe, if only they can find the right mixture of ingredients. You discover the precise ingredients that create successful children; you distill these ingredients to a list of dos and don'ts; you follow the list and re-create the conditions that will lead to a gaggle of Ivy League athletes and subsequent investment bankers. You then get to retire—theoretically happy and content.

Modern metaphors for parenting, as evidenced by the legion of parenting advice books, employ the same language to describe raising children as auto-repair manuals or investing brochures or cookbooks. This is the language of reductive reason, that is, the language of logic and analysis at its most simplistic. If we use simplistic analytic patterns to talk about our kids, we will eventually forge simplistic, sterile, and reductive relationships with them. Notice how many parenting advice books organize their ideas into "bullet points." The bullet point is one of the formatting tools writers use to boil down their complex subjects to digestible bites. The visual metaphor of a bullet speaks for itself.

How many children do you know who can be reduced to a set of bullet points? Whose relationship with their child can be organized into the frames of a PowerPoint presentation? My concern is not that the children themselves will be harmed by the simplistic language and methodologies of parenting books. Children are resilient and free and wonderfully individualistic. The problem is that the language of the parent advice industry is not rich enough to give parents the vocabulary to appreciate and behold their children in all of their miraculous complexity, ambiguity, and holiness. Given the paltry quivers of books that are composed of mere lists, parents may miss the mark of their child. Philosophers and poets have long argued that the words we use to describe the world create the world that we experience. Poetic, religious, and serious scientific vocabularies lend us a multiplicity of hues that help us to experience the world with reverence and awe.

Reductive, elementary guidelines about parenting give us a two-dimensional world; they are also inaccurate. The same parents who gobble up and quote parenting advice books will also tell you that parenting is difficult because it is an activity that refuses to yield to analytic advice—which is why, paradoxically, we buy these books, for we all seek a secure, safe, and understandable port in the storm. My wife is a breast cancer specialist. She often says that the benefit of being a working mother is that her professional life gives her a sense of competence. As a physician, she feels like she knows something. As a mother, she feels helpless and ignorant. Anyone who has parented for even just one night understands that there are no rules or recipes. You are nurturing a being who is a free and distinct individual. Parenting might be more like a craft—say, modeling clay—but only if we imagine each piece of clay to be absolutely unique and inclined to follow its own form no matter our daily and diligent kneading.

In response to the unpredictable nature of children, the effective parents I have witnessed in my career are pragmatists—they use aspects of each parenting style mentioned above as called for by the moment at hand. One case may necessitate the need to follow their duty, while another may call on them to compare and contrast how they were brought up, while at other times they know to sit back and admire the beauty of their children and allow them to develop according to their own logic and passions. We all need a tool bag of different approaches.

This book seeks to flesh out a portrait of the religious parent. I am not claiming to be a religious parent or a parent who knows any more than you do about parenting. I can, though, describe the vision that I yearn for as a parent, even though I rarely am able or wise enough to enact it. One can write about mysticism without being a mystic. When the Trappist monk and writer Thomas Merton visited a Buddhist monastery in Thailand he asked its abbot the meaning of the phrase, "knowledge of freedom." In essence, Father Merton was inquiring about the meaning of enlightenment, and the abbot responded: "When you are in Bangkok, you know that you're there. Before that you only knew about Bangkok. One must ascend all of the steps, but then when there are no more steps one must make the leap. Knowledge of freedom is the knowledge, the experience, of this leap."

I have not been to Bangkok nor have I made the leap. I have, through my work as a headmaster and my theological training, seen the doorway to a way of being a parent. I have not stepped (or leaped) into the room, as lovely as it looks from the vantage point of its threshold. The religious parent sees children as miracles and uses the language of reverence to guide her understanding and actions. She encounters the ordinary episodes of parenting as instances of the sacred appearing in the profane. The comparative religion scholar Mircea Eliade argued that every religion begins with the experience of the eternal in the finite world. He called this experience a hierophany, which literally means the revelation of the holy. Eliade explained that all religions are attempts to articulate this experience of hierophany. The figure of Jesus, as both God and human in one body, is an example of hierophany, but so are the burning bush in the Hebrew Bible and the agricultural cycle in certain primitive religions and the revelations of Allah to Muhammad.

And so too are our children hierophanies, at least in the eyes of the religious parent. I know of no parent, no matter how controlling, logical, and scientific, who is not struck dumb with awe at the birth of their child. What animates this baby? What makes her go? How can she be so much a part of me and so apart at the same time? Atheists, agnostics, and believers alike see a baby as more than just a union of cells. They cannot reconstruct a direct causal path from the biological mechanism of conception to the just-born breathing infant pulsating in their arms for the first time. Creating a life does not seem to be the same as making one domino knock down the next and the next and the next in one logical succession. Something else, something free and wild and mysterious intervenes, to make this person come into the world in the most unlikely way. I would submit that every parent at the moment of birth experiences the mystical insight of hierophany. It is in this rapture of beholding without knowing exactly why that the seeds of humility and spirituality, which are the twin foundations of all religions, are sown. This book asks if we can, in the common, daily acts of parenting re-see, re-view, and re-experience the intermixture of the sacred and the profane in our children that was so clearly immanent at their birth.

One of the teachers at my school told me that as her father neared death after a long illness, he could communicate only by squeezing her hand. She peppered him with as many questions as she could fit into the last minutes of his long life. When she asked if he still had faith, he looked at her and squeezed her hand. She told me that she silently thanked God for "another divine moment." At the end of a life, each minute takes on a special poignancy. In every funeral I have ever attended, I have heard friends and family recount how the seemingly trivial moments of their beloved's final days revealed the very nature of their character.

We can just as easily uncover the spiritual poignancy in the beginning stages of life. What if we had to write a eulogy for our child at the end of each day we spent as a parent? Would we be able to locate the sacred, revelatory moments in the mundane routines we perform each day? Can we see the soul of our children in the way they picked at their peas at dinner? How can we, as parents, locate the divine moments in each frustrating, taxing day of begging our children to eat just a little more, to use an inside voice, to be nice to their sister, to take a nap, to clean up after themselves, to let mommy and daddy talk a little bit, to take a bath, to not draw on the walls?

Chapter 10 of the Chinese mystical masterpiece the *Tao Tê Ching* asks the same question:

> Can your mind penetrate every corner of the land, but you
>   yourself never interfere?
> Rear them, then, feed them,
> Rear them, but do not lay claim to them.
> Control them, but never lean upon them;
> Be chief among them, but do not manage them.
> This is called the Mysterious Power.

Let us explore this mysterious power, so palpable at the moment of birth and so fleeting for the rest of our days until they begin to come to an end. If we set before us the task of beholding one divine moment a day as we rear our children, what might we find and how might that massage a fundamental change into our spiritual sinews as parents?

I am not an enlightened parent, and I struggle each day. I get bored and irritated. I rush right by the most exquisite of moments and the most obvious of revelations. Mystics of all religions teach us that spirituality is a matter of daily practice. We must learn to stop. Walter Kaufmann once said that the great Hasidic scholar Martin Buber taught him that the central commandment of religion is to make the secular sacred. The central commandment of the religious parent is therefore to make the secular aspects of rearing children into opportunities to experience the sacred. I know that as a dad I miss out all the time on reconnecting with the very ground of being. I often cannot come to terms with the basic paradox of parenting, which is also the paradox of faith, namely, that we are ultimately responsible for that which is not within our control. This is the very hard truth of raising a child, and yet, if we could get comfortable with this unfair conundrum, we just might be liberated by it. I write, then, as a fellow traveler, searching, on the way, but a far way, from the majesty of a pure religious practice of parenting. This book, then, is as much for me as it is for you.

I realize that I have been reductive and simplistic in drawing a line between practical, scientific approaches to parenting and the religious sensibility. There is a tension in the history of gardening between naturalistic gardens and formal, ornamental gardens. Naturalism, which was popular in eighteenth-century England as well as in Buddhist India and China, let a grove grow wild with only mild, light gardening touches of planned color and design. A horticultural architect, on the other hand, strictly engineers formal gardens. The bonsai tree typifies this approach, as the gardener carefully restricts water supply and contorts the branches with wire in order to produce the desired shape and height. I could, therefore, have titled this book *The Wild English Garden and the Bonsai Tree: Escaping the Dominant Metaphors of Parenting.* I did not choose this title because there are times when you need to let your child grow according to his or her natural way, and there are times when you must contort their branches with wire. A religious perspective on parenting doesn't choose between the practical and the mystical. Instead, it provides an overarching backdrop of meaning and value supporting the specific techniques we may use and decisions we may make as we parent our children.

I was sincere in my homage to the trio of nurses who wrote the *What to Expect* books. When your child has croup in the middle of the night and is barking like a sick seal, I will be the first to urge you to stop meditating, put the baby in the car, roll the windows down, and go for a drive. This has always done the trick for us, and you will find that your neighborhood has a whole nightlife to it that you never knew existed. A religious perspective on parenting is not meant to displace the bag of tricks and warning signs every parent should know. It is also not offered as a new bag of tricks. Instead, I mean to introduce a parenting sensibility that might give context to the daily dramas of bringing up children. To use two hackneyed academic phrases, a reverential approach to parenting might give us a "lens" through which to view our work as parents that would enable us to "make meaning" of this often maddening work. At the very least, I hope that we can articulate certain aspects of parenting that don't get mentioned or discussed in most of the parenting advice literature.

Even mystery needs some structure and ours will be a simple one. Religion is the articulation of the experience of the ultimate mystery as it reveals itself in the everyday world. Often, this articulation becomes institutionalized into a system of rituals, texts, teachings, and practices. Despite thousands of years of human attempts across all cultures to systematize the experience of the sacred, the mystery continues to elude our grasp. In the same way, despite reams of pages of advice and study and experimentation, the experience of parenting is still a glorious mystery. It is the surprise of the spirit akin to the sometimes shocking and sometimes playful experience we have with the divine.

This book attempts to look at a few things we do daily as parents as instances of the revelation of the divine. Each chapter of the book seeks out a potential hierophany in the life of a typical parent. I ask one question over and over again: How can I learn to appreciate the sacred quality of my role as a parent when I am performing the often grindingly boring chores of raising children? How can I experience the Eternal when I am driving my kids to school or changing their diapers or drawing the boundaries of acceptable behavior? These are the opportunities for parents and those who spend their days with children to behold the spirit, to access the mystery, to feel connected with something profound and greater than our selves, to think beyond, to engage in a truly spiritual moment.

The very nature of the sacred dooms this book to failure, for it is ever elusive, a wisp of smoke slipping through my fingers. I hope, though, that it begins a reverie in a summer's twilight as you watch your children try to eke out one more minute of play before the sun goes down. Being a parent is like driving a car with only a limited dashboard or a torn roadmap. As I stated above, the paradoxical message of each of the world's religions is that though the nature of reality is beyond your personal control, you are still responsible for your world and for your soul. This is the line of tension for every parent. As the Kath-Upanishad from the Hindu tradition states: "Awake, arise! Strive for the Highest, and be in the Light! Sages say the path is narrow and difficult to tread, narrow as the edge of a razor." Instead of trying to avoid or deny or blunt the razor's edge of parenting with checklists and manuals, let's feel what it's like to crawl along it.

2

$\mathcal{K}$nowing

In *Walden*, Thoreau writes "Say what you have to say, not what you ought. Any truth is better than make-believe." He wasn't addressing parents, but this is the best piece of child-rearing advice I've read in a long time. The mission of parenting is to discover the truth of your individual child—not the truth as you want it to be or the truth as you think it ought to be, but the truth as it is in and for itself in the core of the child's being, naked, stark, and beyond your control.

Most fields have their buzzwords that are only understandable to specialists. Priests speak of ecclesiology; doctors study epidemiology. Philosophers of education are no different. One of our favorite words is epistemology. Don't be put off by that term. It relates to the basic questions of knowledge that confront parents and teachers each day.

Picture the following scenario. You and your spouse are in the kitchen, discussing what to have for dinner. Your two sons, Danny, age 3, and Tommy, age 6, are in the family room, battling for a hockey puck. Their laughter provides a pleasant background hum to your conversation, though you can't see the boys. Suddenly, you hear Danny shriek and cry. You both run into the family room and see Danny crumpled on the carpet while Tommy continues to swing at the puck with his plastic hockey stick, calling the play-by-play like an ESPN commentator, completely oblivious to Danny's distress. Your first reaction is probably to rush to Danny's side to see if he is bleeding or injured. When you see that he is okay, you step back and ask, "What happened?"

Assuming that, as I guarantee will be the case, Danny and Tommy give conflicting explanations, you face a problem that has plagued the minds of philosophers and theologians since the dawn of cognition—how to acquire knowledge and know the truth, or what is really happening. If you have ever been uncertain and wondered how to make the right decision, you're an epistemologist.

Epistemology is the branch of philosophy that asks questions about the nature of knowledge and truth. Is certain knowledge ever attainable? If so, how? If not, how can we ever know how to make a decision? Is rationality the only way to know that something is true? What about gut feelings, faith, and emotion? Do we always need evidence to believe something is so? What kinds of evidence?

These questions confront parents and teachers each day, especially in seemingly insignificant circumstances. For example, as the parent of Tommy and Danny, you probably begin with an investigation, being careful to observe due process. Through his tears, Danny blubbers that his brother speared him in the gut. After first ignoring your question entirely and continuing his hockey pantomime, Tommy says that Danny tripped and it was his own fault. In a flash, Danny turns to Tommy, accuses him of lying, and then attempts to verbally spear him back by stating that he hates Tommy, he has always hated Tommy, and he always will hate Tommy.

You, as the rationalist, now come to the limits of procedural justice. You have two accounts; since they contradict each other, they cannot both be true. The epistemologist in you acknowledges that this would be an easier situation if Danny was bleeding from the alleged spearing, but the parent in you is relieved there are no marks, cuts, or bruises. So now you are in the unpleasant realm of uncertainty. You don't know what happened, and, indeed, you can never know for certain, ever. So what now? Ignore the event?

One solution is a rule-based approach, to establish a general principle to make the messiness of this situation tidier. You might say, "From this day forward, Tommy, as the older brother, I hold you responsible for whatever happens to Danny. After all, he's only three." Parents do this all the time, trying to formalize family conflicts for all occasions by creating the equivalent of an employee manual of a small business. We make policy pronouncements and set up procedures and vow to never stray from them, so help us. Then, of course, we amend them the next day. The sloppiness of life never fits the neat contours of our generalizations.

~

We never see God directly through the window,
because we are always painting pictures on the
window itself.

~

Instead of setting rules, you might decide to go with your intuition. Tommy has a history of tormenting his little brother. Just the other day, as a matter of fact, you had to rescue Danny from Tommy's lasso. Actually, Tommy has always been jealous of his little brother. Everyone pays attention to Danny—he is cute, and frankly, he's showing more promise as an athlete than Tommy. You might understand Tommy's feelings if you, too, were the older sibling. Using Tommy's resentment as your guiding theme, you conclude that Tommy did indeed spear his brother (after all, you'd done similar things to your little brother), so you put him in a time-out. Of course, Tommy screams from his jail cell in the dining room. "It's not fair!" arguing, something to the effect, using his limited vocabulary, that you have reneged on your duty to pure procedural justice. You acted irrationally in the absence of hard facts and have simply become a sloppy epistemologist.

You wonder if Tommy just might be right.

You could take other approaches as well. You could become a radical skeptic. Since you can never be 100 percent sure what happened, why even bother asking the boys what happened? After all, for all you know they might both be lying. Or you could simply adopt a relativist position, stating that there are many truths depending on the observer, and then just beg the two boys to be quiet, for heaven's sake.

Such positions work better in theory than in practice. The history of philosophy began with a quest for certainty and, failing in that quest, has resolved itself in the present day with theories to help us live with uncertainty. We parents are an interesting brand of epistemologists, for we are not theorists. We must act and make decisions even though we're always uncertain. If you adopted a purely skeptical position, it would be impossible to get out of bed in the morning, much less raise children.

The Tommy/Danny story represents a small episode in the daily drama of a family. Knowing your children and knowing the way to know your children involves much more than questions about evidence and procedures. To simplify, there are two basic kinds of knowledge: knowing about something and knowing something.

Knowing about involves a distanced objectivity as well as our ability to accumulate facts and general principles over time. Knowing something per se involves an almost mystical union with the thing that is known. This type of knowledge is beyond facts and linguistic formula. It also discards ideas that we might impose on the world, and, instead, allows us direct access to another being. Thus, mechanics know about carburetors, but no mechanic knows carburetors, unless, that is, she is a mystical mechanic. The theologian Alan Watts once pointed out that we never see God directly through the window, because we are always painting pictures on the window itself, understanding the pictures as the really real. The kind of knowing I am talking about is equivalent to the attachment reserved for certain ecstatic spiritual experiences, both joyful and sad. It happens when you gaze in your newborn's eyes for the first time. It occurs when you feel their pain as your own in the emergency room, as a tube is inserted down their nostril to inject dye for the CT scan.

I invite you to look at the journey of parenting as both coming to know about and coming to know your child. Parenting knowledge is a balance between objectivity and unity. The joy and the miracle of rearing children is found not only in getting to know them as individuals separate from you, the parent, but also in the fact that you change and grow along with your children. This is both thrilling and sobering—it's fun to be on the adventure with them, but children may have aspects that horrify you, and they may show you, in explicit and unexpected ways, the less attractive parts of your personality.

The other day, my wife and I and another couple were watching our four children romp in their backyard. Each one of the adults had an Ivy League degree, and we were discussing how we were dealing with the reality of our careers. Each of us had dreamed of great success, but we had not yet achieved our youthful aspirations. Our wives were quite comfortable with this reality, while the other husband and I were discussing how we would probably never be satisfied. Later, we began to comment on how competitive our children were with each other and with their siblings about possessing toys and winning board games. This daily competition, we agreed, was such a drag, and we wondered where our children picked up their drive to dominate the toy room and the playground. We paused, looked at each other, and finally laughed, for of course our children's playground behavior was just a deadly accurate echo of who we really were as adults—competitive perfectionists.

Thoreau's advice to speak the truth instead of make-believe implies that it is sometimes painful to speak the truth. Many parents use fiction as a roadmap for parenting. But fiction, even entertaining fiction, often undercuts reality and truth. Knowing the really real takes a lot of work. It's always easier to write our own narrative about our children—make-believe stories where they are dressed up in innocence or always made to follow a script we've written for them.

There are two pitfalls when we make fictions of our children. One, it does violence to our kids because we don't allow them to blossom as individuals. And two, it does violence to others—parents and educators run into problems when one group clings too faithfully to the fictions they have created.

As a headmaster, I often hear from parents that the troubling behavior we are reporting at school has never been observed in the home environment. For example, we once had a second grader who was caught stealing and cheating. At first, his parents did dispute the facts of the case. "Our little girl does not steal," they said. As the incidents multiplied and the girl began to confess, almost compulsively, her parents offered an interpretation that cast a different light on the situation. Her parents blamed the teacher. According to them, the teacher was so academically demanding that she created an atmosphere of anxiety, crushing the poor girl's ability to know right from wrong.

In their family script, their child, left to her own instincts, was incapable of immoral behavior. Hence, immorality must have come from some toxic element in the school's atmosphere. (Perhaps not so ironically, these same parents were successful, demanding, academic careerists.) As a headmaster I was, of course, frustrated by their behavior, but as a parent I completely understood the trap they had fallen into. Their mistake was in not following Thoreau's dictum to avoid the make-believe. These parents had the opportunity to be epistemologists, always seeking more and more data for an ever-expanding understanding of their child in all of her unpredictable messiness, good and bad. Instead, they clung to a family myth. They expressed the arrogance of a closed mind rather than the humility of a discovering mind.

As parents, overworked and sleep-deprived, we often want truth to be final, and even more importantly, we want peace and quiet at the end of the day. Thoreau's distinction between make-believe and truth is not a simple distinction between hallucinations and facts. With the word "ought," Thoreau implies that we have a moral duty to sincerely seek out truth and speak it when we know it. We do not have a duty, on the other hand, to conform to the expectations of others or our preformed notions. Codified principles and inherited expectations are just as much make-believe as stories and poems. The problem with make-believe is that it is a self-contained, detached, and limited universe. Novels and short stories have endings; parenting, at least the part of parenting that is the deliberate quest to come to know your child, never ends. It is exhausting, but never exhaustive or exhausted.

One interesting fact about the history of knowledge is that the nature of our quest for certainty is always changing. For Thoreau, knowledge and truth were more of a disposition to remain open to an understanding of how all things are connected. Instead of stamping a preconceived concept onto reality, Thoreau provokes us to constantly attend and experiment. He wants us to hold and to behold the child. This is what parents who expect the unexpected do—and they revel in the process even in its pain and uncertainty. Tommy's howls for justice just might provoke a new interpretation of the episode. While he must learn not to spear his brother's spleen, his parents might also come to understand that his plight to find his place in the world, and his thirst for justice, might need some tending. Until dinner time that is, when the peas start flying.

3

Disappointing

My six-year-old attended a Christmas party that, in addition to a visit from Santa Claus, featured hundreds of balloons strewn across an indoor tennis court. The children played all sorts of games with the balloons. At the end of the party, the children were invited to pop the balloons using sharpened pencils. Since there weren't enough pencils to go around, the children resorted to stomping on the balloons. Imagine the echoing explosions of hundreds of bursting balloons as the children gleefully destroyed as many as they could. Afterward, the green court was strewn with shredded, multicolored latex corpses.

My son happily contributed to the carnage, but I noticed that in the men's locker room he'd safely hidden one red balloon. When we left the party, he carried that balloon to the car, cradling it in his arms and taking great pains to keep it away from sharp objects—and his younger brother. Back at home, he put the balloon in the family room and for two days made it his constant plaything, keeping a record of how many times he could tap it in the air without letting it fall to the ground. After each session, he treated the balloon with great respect and reverence and carefully put it away in a safe corner of his room.

During the day, however, the balloon inevitably scooted out of his room, bounded across the stairwell, and landed on top of a tall china cabinet in our foyer. Henry asked me to get it down for him, and I decided to make it into a thinking game.

I said, "Why don't you *persuade* the balloon to come down, instead of just grabbing it."

Henry looked at me impatiently.

I tried again. "Tell the balloon why it will be good for the balloon, not just for you, to come down from the cabinet."

You could see in Henry's eyes that he was slowly getting my point.

He said, "Come down, balloon. I want to play with you."

"But give the balloon a reason he would *want* to play with you," I coached.

Henry winced and whined, "Da-a-a-ady, I just want to play with the balloon. Will you pleeeease get it down for me?" I tried one more time. "Pretend the balloon is a person. Explain to him why it's fun for him to have you poke him in the head with your fingers over and over again so that his head bobs up and down. Henry, would you want someone to jab at your head over and over again?"

"Okay. Balloon, if you come down, I can make you fly, and flying is fun, so come down," Henry enticed the balloon.

I beamed. I swooned. My son was learning how to spin, how to sell, how to persuade. "You did it, Henry." He was going to be a politician someday. Or a CEO. I grabbed the red balloon for him.

Later that day Henry, out of nowhere, asked: "Why did you make me say those silly things to the balloon? I just wanted to play with it."

"I wanted you to think about the balloon and see things from his point of view," I said.

"Why?"

"Because thinking is good and you came up with a very good reason for the balloon to come down. If you thought it was so silly, why did you come up with such a good thought?"

"Because I didn't want to disappoint you, Dad. I still think it was silly."

Henry caught me short with this. He was telling me that I'd embarrassed him. I'd forced him to play a game I wanted to play, one that he found slightly undignified. In philosophical terms, I had treated Henry as a means to my end, that is, as a way to achieve my goals and not his goals. I hadn't taken him on his own terms, as his own person. He was also telling me that he feared disappointing me. Henry realized, though, that to please me, he may have to, at times, subvert his desires. He reminded me that disappointment is a potent and potentially dangerous parental tool.

I should've remembered this. When I tell my son that his behavior has disappointed me, he crumples like a piece of cellophane. He would far prefer a concrete punishment or a simple tongue-lashing than the deflating words of disappointment. And he's not the only one to feel this way. Many of my friends and colleagues have told me similar stories about their childhood. The worst thing they could do, beyond the consequences and moral implications of their actions, was to disappoint their parents. A friend told me that, once late at night on a back road, he totaled the family car after swerving to avoid running into a deer. Though relieved that he and his passenger had escaped injury, the sight of the crumpled metal frightened him, and he worried about the insurance and replacement costs. Yet he didn't feel any emotional anguish until his father said, "Son, I'm very disappointed in you." He then broke down and cried.

What's going on here? Why, for some children, does "disappointing" a parent hurt worse than being given a time-out or performing a difficult chore? Why do parents utter such a potent word as "disappointment"? Are parents and children doomed to disappoint each other? If so, what does this say about the nature of family relationships?

The disappointment issue helps us highlight important moral and spiritual elements in parenting. The word "disappoint" originally meant to fire someone; it meant, literally, to remove him or her from his or her official appointment. It has since come to mean a kind of sad and weary frustration. I think, though, that when a child feels that she has disappointed her father, she hears the original roots of the word. She fears that she has been disappointed—removed from her position in the family as a beloved child. It's a sickening feeling of alienation. She questions her identity and her status. She realizes that her entire life, which up to this moment had seemed so safe and solid, was always provisional. When her father says that she has disappointed him, she feels that she has always been on trial. In effect, when a child disappoints her parents, she begins to understand the conditions of her par-

~

When you choose the soft language of disappointment, your child may start to live his life trying to avoid disappointing you.

~

ents' love. This love, it is revealed, has boundaries. Disappointment demarcates the property lines of familial acceptance and affection. By probing this boundary, our children begin to feel queasy, because what they took to be eternal and endless turns out to be contingent. Disappointing mom or dad shakes your foundations and leads you to understand that these foundations were always shifting, never solid.

When parents say, after their teenager wrecks the family car in a drunken stupor, "I'm not angry with you; I'm disappointed in you," do they mean to alienate him? Probably not. If you ask them, most parents will explain that they really only intended to distinguish the child's behavior from the child's essential self. It's a "hate the sin, love the sinner" kind of argument. From this point of view, to be disappointed in someone is actually a compliment. It means that I know the real you. The real you is a fine, honest, responsible young man. There is also a fake you—an unreal you—who sometimes gives into peer pressure, takes my car keys, buys cheap beer, guzzles it with his friends, puts everyone's life in danger, and finally destroys the family car. To express disappointment in this case is to try to create a partnership between the parent and the real child in an effort to eradicate the unreal child who does all of these terrible deeds. The parent chooses to respond with disappointment instead of anger in order to avoid pointless battles.

Rage and punishment are militaristic responses that many feel are too violent and inappropriate; disappointment is a mode of parenting that seems more gentle and diplomatic. But it's easy to fall into a troubling spiritual trap when you choose the seemingly softer language of disappointment, because your child may start to live his life trying to avoid disappointing you. Take the case of my son and the red balloon. He was more afraid of disappointing me than participating in what was, to him, an embarrassing game. Why is this a spiritual trap? When we tell our daughter that she has disappointed us, we aren't authentically engaging her as a full human being who is free and separate from us as an individual in her own right. The relationship between the disappointer and the disappointed is not a reciprocal one or a mutually respectful one. That "real self"—that deeper, essential self we think we are honoring—is a projection of our parental fantasies. We slice the whole child into parts to be accepted and rejected, leaving the child feeling fractured and alienated from an authentic relationship with the parent.

The German philosopher Immanuel Kant said that the source of all moral thinking should be founded on the following proposition: "Man and generally any rational being exists as an end in himself, not merely as a means to be arbitrarily used by this or that will, but in all his actions, whether they concern himself or other rational beings, must be always regarded at the same time as an end." In order to enjoy a moral relationship, we must respect the integrity and dignity of each person we encounter. When we are disappointed in our child, we treat them as a means to our personal ends and desires.

In other words, when we are disappointed in our children, we don't respect their freedom and their individuality. We don't acknowledge that they are authentic human beings with their own wills pointing them toward their unique destinies. One of the shocks of parenthood is the realization that your child is separate from you. The path of maturation leads from absolute physical intimacy in the womb, to the intense physical intimacy of caring for an infant, to the intensely private distance of an adolescent roaming the rafters of your house.

This does not imply, as certain liberal parenting manuals suggest, that we ought to let our children drift off like a stick on a river swept along by every current. Freedom and authenticity doesn't mean that everything ought to be allowed. As Walter Kaufmann wisely reminds us, Kant's formulation does not preclude the fact that we sometimes do, and must, treat other people as a means to our ends. The key phrases in Kant's proposition are "not merely as" and "at the same time." In order to survive we must sometimes treat another individual merely as a means. I have a bullet wound in my chest, and you are a doctor. I am lost, and you have a map. The kitchen is a mess, and I have a nasty flu and need you to help me by cleaning your room. When I do treat you as a means, I must at the same time respect that you are ultimately a person who, by the mere fact of your humanity, is free and worthy of respect and dignity.

One night we were driving home from a particularly stressful extended family gathering. My sons must have picked up on the stress, because they were going out of their way to annoy each other in the back seat. Spencer would yank a toy from Henry's hand; Henry would scream "unfair!" Henry would regain the toy; Spencer would cry and then pound back with his fists. My wife and I tried to reason with them. "We'll be home shortly." "Let's just get through this ride." Then we tried threats. "We'll take away your toys." "Santa Claus is still keeping a list of naughty and nice boys for next year." We tried to soothe them with inane but mesmerizing children's music.

Nothing worked. The territorial backseat battle between two brothers raged on.

Without thinking, and in an instant, I lost it. I told them to shut up (a phrase I strenuously try to avoid). I swore. I said that I hated the way they were acting, and that they would be separated as soon as they got home. My voice was guttural, loud, and primitive. Instantly, the boys fell silent. Then Spencer started to cry, softly, into the corner of his car seat. I could tell that my wife was "disappointed" in me as she sulked deeper into the passenger seat. I felt terrible, and yet I must admit, the silence was delicious. I played back the scene in my head, like a football coach watching game films on Monday morning, and asked myself what other techniques I could have used.

Eventually the boys perked up and started to amicably chatter. They even came up with their own scheme to encourage them to be better behaved in the car. Starting with five dollars, they suggested we take away a dollar for every time they fought. They would get whatever money was left over at the end of the car ride. (The deal fell through when they realized that if they fought more than five times, they would owe me money.)

I decided that every once in a while, it is helpful, in fact, respectful, to lose your temper, as long as you are aware of what you are doing and deliberate in your use of your anger. If anger is not your natural state of being, then when you do lose it, you're actually stating, in effect, "we are in this together." What you do affects me, and it affects the climate of the home. In Buber's terms, there is no more an I without a You—and right now, as You both treat each other as Its, You have hurt me and us. I'm not disappointed in you; I am angry with you. I am angry with you because I am connected to you. I am angry with you because I love you.

4

$\mathcal{P}$laying

PROGRESSIVE EDUCATORS TELL US THAT "PLAY IS A CHILD'S work." This was once considered a radical statement, but it has come to articulate an uncontroversial truth for most parents and schools. I have never visited a kindergarten or early childhood education center that didn't support this idea. Indeed, teachers of older children and adolescents are now considered good or bad, not only by the children but by their parents, according to how

~

To say that play is work is almost to apologize for play.

~

much "play" they use to introduce more conceptual subject matter. Lecturing and answering questions from a textbook are now considered poor teaching methods. Teachers are considered inventive and creative if they use games and activities to help children learn about molecules, modifiers, and Madagascar. In the modern American school, play is no longer just a child's work—it's adult work as well.

One of my colleagues told me about a complaint he received at Parent Information Night at the school where he serves as headmaster. At this event, a teacher is allotted eight minutes to explain to parents the goals, the content, and the materials of her courses. This particular parent—we'll call her Mrs. Stone—thought the science teacher was particularly boring, droning on as he read verbatim from his syllabus. Mrs. Stone was afraid that if he was this dull in the classroom, he would kill her daughter's love of science.

Mrs. Stone's older son was attending another school. At parent night, the science teacher passed out a box containing an unnamed object. The parents were instructed to use their five senses and deductive reasoning powers to determine the nature of the hidden object. Mrs. Stone admitted afterwards that she had only a vague idea of the exact subject matter of her son's course. But the box exercise had proven to her that her son's teacher was exciting and innovative.

Mrs. Stone makes a valid point. Teachers need to engage their students to be thrilled by the prospect of learning. But things can go too far. Our obsession with making work into play disrespects play and reduces it to the instrumental purposes of work. It also doesn't teach our children to be tolerant of drudgery, which is a fact of any life. To say that play is work is almost to apologize for play—"see, play really does accomplish something." Cutting with scissors is no longer about the joy of shaping a form out of a blank state; the child is really honing his fine motor skills. It's good for boys and girls to play soccer on a recess field, because they're developing gross motor skills and learning how to cooperate in a team setting. Building a castle with blocks and populating it with pipe cleaner sculptures of dragons and knights helps build the imagination. Imaginative play helps develop creative problem-solving skills, which children will need later in life when they take on leadership positions.

I don't deny that motor and cognitive skill developments are by-products of children's play. But play is also a spiritual mode of being in and for itself. It is spiritual for many reasons, but most importantly it is a holistic experience for the child, one that engages her whole being. When a child plays, she uses all of her faculties. The physical, the emotional, the cognitive, and the spiritual are undivided and unselfconsciously employed. The playing child's totality of attention is the epitome of spiritual enlightenment.

Observe your four-year-old daughter playing. Say it's Christmas day. She kneels before the tree as if in supplication. The boxes are all unwrapped, and her various gifts are scattered under the tree and across the floor. She's an interdisciplinary player. Her plastic pandas climb aboard the black-striped safari truck and ride through the jungle of string and colored petals and glue tubes from her arts-and-crafts box. The pandas then dismount, scamper up a large rubber ball and assemble in a neat line on the windowsill, where they watch her older cousin chase a football on the front lawn. The pandas cheer on the cousin, but also mock him with wild delight when he misses the ball and slips on the wet, muddy sod. Suddenly, the pandas are abandoned, and your daughter saunters over to a table strewn with heads and wigs and hands and bodies and feet. She begins to construct a collection of grotesque creatures. Some have green bodies and huge heads of hair, some have tiny heads and a ponytail held in place by a bone. Taking a pen, she draws a house with a couch and a lamp, then settles this group in for the day.

If you watch her surreptitiously, you notice her complete lack of self-consciousness. Your house is full of relatives and the tensions of the holidays, yet your daughter is serenely alone. She is totally absorbed. It's almost as if she is in a trance, except that she is in complete control of her world. Indeed, she is creating a world. Her breathing is slow and steady. Her mind and her body and her toys are one. An athlete would call this being in the zone. An artist would identify a similar state of consciousness in the creative process. A Taoist would recognize, in the blending of mind, body, spirit, and world, the way and the power of the Tao, that mysterious, harmonious power of the universe in which all contradictions and opposites are healed and blended.

The play of young children resembles something so much more profound than merely rehearsing for more mature grown-up tasks. If you ask your daughter what she is doing, you'll break her trance, but she will patiently tell you a story. Delighted to be given the role of sage and raconteur, she will tell you what ought to be obvious. A pack of pandas goes for a ride and they get caught up in some yarn but they get out and watch the silly boy fall down in the mud and then this weird family moves into their house. Her stories about what she just played are almost always in the present tense, giving them a timeless, eternal quality. Play is a parallel universe that keeps on occurring even after the child stops to explain what has just happened.

If you reflect on it all—the slowed breath, the forgetfulness, the bent knees, the oneness of subject and object (child and toy), the intense concentration, the blissful expression—the religious parent recognizes the meditative and spiritual aspects of a child's play. Meister Eckhart's term, the "now-moment," which describes the mystical relationship when a person and God are one and transcend linear time, also illustrates the state of the child at play. With their intense concentration, children at play exhibit an enlightened state of mind that Buddhists call being "wide-awake," where every aspect of a person's being is integrated—on point— and still relaxed.

Parents often notice that their children are more interested in the box the toy came in than the toy itself. That is because a child inhabits an imaginative universe; a toy as a toy restricts the freedom of his mind, forcing him to conform to the limits of the toy's maker. The box can become anything, even a space ship. At heart, children are postmodernists, loving to blend genres and cross boundaries. Civil War soldiers cozy up to polar bears and wade through iceberg fields of balled up scotch tape, only to be netted by huge wads of wrapping paper.

Philosophers and poets throughout the ages have extolled the spiritual qualities of the imagination. The poet-philosopher Samuel Taylor Coleridge distinguished between the primary and the secondary imaginations. Coleridge believed that we re-create the world with each act of perception. God has created the basic stuff of the world, but every time we see this stuff (or hear, smell, touch, or taste it), we activate this stuff and organize it into a coherent field of understanding. In this way, Coleridge held that each human is a co-creator with God. He labeled these basic acts of perception "primary imagination."

Another kind of cognition called the "secondary imagination" energizes the artistic parts of the self. This kind of imagination illuminates the deeper senses of creation. Secondary imagination does not "make things up" as the term "imaginary" might imply. When Picasso puts handlebars on top of a bicycle seat, creating the head of a bull, he pushes beyond the mere given and reconfigures reality. Yet his sculpture is firmly grounded in real things. Those are real handlebars and that is a hard and fast seat. He teaches the observer to break the habits of perception and see the world in a new way. Coleridge and many other thinkers recognize a mode of spirituality at work in the acts of the secondary imagination, because of its participation in the creation of the world as we might experience it. As we see the world anew, we renew it and ourselves. As we renew, we refresh and even redeem.

William Blake, another celebrant of the imagination, wrote, in his poem "Milton," about a place called Beulah, where "Contrarieties are equally True." Beulah, which is a metaphor for the creative impulse, is also a Taoist playground, where the imagination harmonizes what would normally be taken as exclusive contradictions. In the artistic consciousness, the human reflection of God's consciousness, life and death, soccer balls and billiard balls, light and dark, dolls and army men, men and women, fire trucks and medieval knights, wet and dry, tall and short, and bears and race cars can coexist and make sense together without irony or absurdity.

This kind of vision represents the healing work of God's grace, where the seemingly incompatible come together. The secondary imagination is, in a way, an expression of grace, for it heals oppositions. In Beulah, Blake sings, "It is a pleasant lovely Shadow/ Where no dispute can come, because of those who Sleep." Those who sleep are dreaming and those who dream escape the boundaries and bondage of logic. Sleepers are, in a way, more free than those who are wide awake. The play of a child resembles this kind of redemptive sleep not only because of the near trance we witness when we see our three-year-old before a tower of blocks. They may as well be asleep; we cannot gain their attention to come to the door to put on their coat. Your son has transcended the traditional distance between subject and object as he seeks to balance one more block on the tower. He is the block; he is the tower.

In addition, your playing child is controlling the given world and through an act of the secondary imagination creating a new universe. In this wholly natural way, she is participating with God the Creator. She may never again be as close in spirit to God as when she throws herself into creative play. And we would be wise to throw ourselves in with her. Yet the traditional road to maturation seeks to teach children to divide the world into "contrarieties." This belongs with that thing, we say, and does not belong with that other thing. School curricula stretch from the integration of the kindergarten day to the abstract segregation of the high school schedule. In early childhood programs, letters and cutting and gluing and math and coloring are all seen as one activity with the body and the mind informing each other. Later, we weed these out for the child. Art period begins as English ends, and art will end when math begins.

So we prod our children to abandon their secondary imaginations in favor of their primary imaginations. To do so, though, is to encourage them to abandon a natural faculty that enables them to participate in creation. Emerson complained that we come to think of the creation as an act that long ago happened. Along with Coleridge, he encouraged us to recognize the creation as a contemporary act that partners people with God. This implies that we are responsible for our world. It is not given to us. We help make it what it is. Play and responsibility, therefore, go hand in hand. The poet and writer Delmore Schwartz entitled one of his short stories "In Dreams Begin Responsibility." This could be the title of this chapter. When we believe that the universe is not given to us by a distant creator, but that we are, minute-by-minute, co-creators of a daily miracle, then we become responsible actors in this world. Play is not escape for the child; it is an entrance into a world where they must take care. The impulse to take care of a world is the root of our deepest religious impulses. It is one of our most important spiritual obligations as parents to encourage play and to find ways for children to retain their imaginative selves, even as they mature and develop logical and analytical habits of thought. The mystical traditions of the world's religions attempt to regain the spiritual gifts of the playing child. If only they could never lose them.

5

$\mathcal{P}$ooping

MY POOPING STORY TAKES PLACE BY THE SIDE OF A pool at a four-star Toronto hotel, where we are surrounded by a bevy of rock and movie stars.

My family lives in Buffalo, New York. Buffalo is a great city in its own right, especially as a place to raise children, but one of its pleasures is its proximity to Toronto. Only an hour-and-a-half drive from downtown Buffalo, Toronto has become an international destination, offering as much sophisticated entertainment as London, New York, San Francisco, and Paris. Even better, for many years the American dollar was very strong against Canadian currency, so some Buffalonians of modest means could upgrade their normal vacation plans by traveling to Toronto and getting to stay at a luxurious hotel like the Four Seasons.

One early summer weekend, my family did just that. My sons were five and two at the time. After we checked in and the boys fulfilled their need to bounce from bed to bed, we met our friends for an afternoon at the hotel pool. The crowd at the pool was an eclectic mix of middle-class families like us and gorgeous young women in skimpy bikinis. I then noticed a man resembling Charlie Watts strolling over to a group of these women. He kneeled before them, chatted, and then stretched out on a deck chair. I asked one the attendants if that man was indeed "the" drummer for the Rolling Stones. He nodded yes, explaining that the Stones were rehearsing in Toronto for their North American tour, and some of them had taken up residence at the Four Seasons. Unable to contain his pride in the hotel, he also mentioned that the movie *The In-Laws* was filming in town, and that some of the cast, including the stars Michael Douglas and Albert Brooks, were in residence.

Just as I was savoring the delicious peculiarity of the Four Seasons's business plan to appeal to midwestern American families and international celebrities at the same time, my son interrupted my reverie, announcing that he had to use the potty. I escorted him to the pool's shower and locker room. I waited at the door (hoping to catch a glance of Keith or Mick) when I heard my son screaming over and over again, "Daddy, will you wipe me?"

I rushed back into the locker room to minister to him when I ran right into Albert Brooks, who was also rushing toward my son's stall. Mr. Brooks looked at me and said something like, "How did my son get down here? He's supposed to be in the room with my wife! Now where is he?" I told him it was actually *my* son who was calling out. Mr. Brooks, clad in a terry cloth bathrobe, immediately plopped down on a bench and observed that all five-year-old boys sound alike. I asked him if his boy still asked to be wiped even though he was potty trained. He acknowledged that his son was the same way. We chatted amicably for a few seconds. Many thoughts were racing through my head. I had always like Mr. Brooks's work in the movies. I had especially identified with his neurotic character in *Broadcast News*. I debated whether to ask him for his autograph, as if to acknowledge that we were not just mere dads, and that he occupied a much more exalted place than I.

I decided to let the moment pass. I introduced my son to Mr. Brooks and then hurried away back to my friends. Charlie Watts was walking out with the bikini-clad women. I excitedly reported to my wife that for one brief moment, Albert Brooks and I had shared a common parenting problem. We collected the kids, dried them off, and fed them dinner by the side of the pool.

In 1832, Ralph Waldo Emerson, who at that time was ailing both spiritually and physically, wrote to his brother, "There is a limit beyond which people's interest in other people's bowels cannot go." Not so for parents. No matter what position you hold in society, if you are a parent, dealing with your child's intestines brings us all down to common ground. Many of my friends before they had children were shy, fastidious, and almost coy about their bodies. Bodily functions were simply not a topic of conversation. After having children, though, we filled our conversations with urine and blood and vomit. Our houses and apartments, once so neatly arranged according to the latest insights of feng shui, now became a mess, smelling like hospital wards. A house with a new baby, like the new baby himself, smells both sweet and sour. The odor of vapor rub provides only a thin, medicinal veneer to cover the pervasive smell of fecal matter. One of my friends, a dandy corporate executive, has even taken to farting freely in front of other people because he can always blame the odor on one of the children.

Psychologists tend to view potty training as a critical stage in the emotional development of young children. As children learn to use the toilet, they also develop the emotion of disgust, as well as the ability to control themselves and, subsequently, others. Some view potty training as the first step in the child's progress toward independence and personal responsibility. Parents familiar with the psychoanalytic tradition face potty training with trepidation, for they fear that they may increase their child's neurotic tendencies if it is not handled in just the right way. If you are very careful, some think, you might just ward off the possibility of an anal-retentive adult, but only if you make the bathroom a fun, relaxed place for your three-year-old. Indeed, some parents think that an entire family history of adult neurotic neatness might just be circumvented with the right approach to potty training.

All of the above are true to a certain extent. When my child refused to yield to the pleasures of the toilet, a friend suggested that we make him responsible for his own soiling. We hung a clothesline in a back bathroom, gave him a pile of clothespins and clean underwear and told him to clean up his own messes. He was trained within a day of handing over the responsibility and power to him. He has been a very responsible little boy since. The same technique did not work, though, on his younger brother. You never know.

Beyond technique and personality development, there is also a spiritual dimension to potty training. Emerson's offhand, sardonic comment about other people's bowels invites an insight into the limits of compassion, for it links spirituality, morality, and our body. Raising a child immerses you in the precinct of the body, for parenting is intensely corporeal. You must be comfortable with excretions of all types emitting from every orifice. You are constantly cleaning and wiping. You now understand and develop a new respect for the daily life of a nurse. You also become so much more comfortable with your own body in its glory and in its malodorous malfunctions. By becoming at home with your body, you become at home with yourself. You accept yourself. What's more, moms and dads of newborns don't have the time to groom as much as they did when they were childless. Make-up and hair gel become less important amenities than the luxury of four hours of uninterrupted sleep. This is spiritually liberating, for as the major world religions teach, acceptance for what is and who we are is the first step toward love and spiritual wisdom.

Even before they are born, children help us fathers toward enlightenment. It is common now for fathers to be present in the delivery room. While wives welcome the support, they also fear that their mate will no longer see them as attractive after witnessing the utter and uncompromising physicality of childbirth. Our second child was delivered by caesarian section. The surgeon on call turned out to be our neighbor, and he immediately put me at ease. He invited me to stay and observe the whole procedure, demonstrating and explaining his techniques as if I were a medical student. He also gave me an internal anatomy lesson. I realized that by turning the process into a scientific lesson, the surgeon had engaged my intellect and lessened my anxiety.

I told my wife about all this afterwards. She is also a physician and so she asked me if, having seen her internal organs, I could still view here romantically (the answer, of course, was yes). It was an important question, for we tend to romanticize people and try not to think too much about the messy parts of their bodily existence.

~

Parenting is intensely corporeal—you are constantly cleaning and wiping.

~

Jesus and Muhammad and Buddha and the Hebrew prophets called for each of us to embrace and love our neighbors as full and complex beings who are composed of both matter and spirit. Having children forces us to adopt this holistic vision. To see beauty in all aspects of your wife is to discover a new level of love—one that, I would argue, is spiritually transformative. And when you raise a child together, you will see each other in all sorts of unflattering situations. Fashion magazines do not feature models who have woken up at 2 AM, thrown on sweats, jeans, and slippers, and driven a child to the emergency room. Parents of newborns love to adorn their homes with photographs of themselves before they had children to remind themselves and visitors that they were once young and beautiful. There they are—tanned and fit on a beach, rugged and determined hiking up a mountain, drunk and carefree at a café in some foreign capital. Yet, when they are forced to accept and love a 360-degree reality of each other, they have broken through the realm of mere appearances and uncovered a deeply religious truth. By returning to the realm of the everyday, parents taste a bit of the eternal.

The corporeal envelope that defines the existence of parents of every young child—evidenced by numerous daily diaper changes, pervasive drool, periodic vomiting, hourly crying, burping, and farting, and anal thermometers lubricated by thick gelatinous petroleum jelly the odor and viscosity of which clings to your fingers for days thereafter—is religious in many ways. It is cyclical, like a daily liturgy. Many passages in the Hebrew Bible characterize humanity as akin to the most abject and disgusting aspects of creation as well as the most exalted. We are dust and maggots, and we are also angels. Similarly, the New Testament does not shy away from the physical reality of human life. The crucifixion is only the most graphic and dramatic illustration of the nexus of body and spirit in Christian theology. The stories of Jesus's ministry are almost always narratives that involve the needs of the body. People throughout the New Testament are sick and thirsty, hungry and bleeding, dusty and sore, blind and ulcerous.

Our child is one minute emitting the most foul of excretions and the next sweetly and warmly cuddling in our arms. The physical reality of our child reminds us that a child is a hierophany. We see our child as a whole being. Though we can intellectually distinguish between her body and her spirit, we experience our child as one. The sacred and the profane are intermingled. As Eliade has explained, this is how religious communities experience and articulate their notions of the divine and the eternal. To paraphrase Bob Dylan, pooping brings us all back home. It reminds us that all of the spiritual feelings we access as parents—love, redemption, mystery, and a touch of eternity—are not somewhere out there, beyond our ken. The powers of the spirit are right here, on earth, and everywhere around us. Your acceptance of and comfort with your child's bodily functions is an invitation to see the whole of existence anew. If you can feel close to the ground of your being by changing a dirty diaper, then you can find God in a cobweb, in a pearl of dew, or in a clod of dirt.

When I was in divinity school, I told one of my professors that I felt close to God when I went for long bike rides in the woods. She said that was all well and good, but the trick was to find God in the inner city, among the impoverished, in bombed-out buildings, among the homeless gathered around burning garbage can hearths. She was right. And in the same way, parenting can teach us to experience the divine in the most profane of places.

There is another way that the omnipresent concerns of your child's body can be seen as religious. Zen Buddhist practice teaches that meditation is not a technique to escape reality but to accept it and to come to terms with it. By sitting still for hours and disciplining our minds to concentrate on what is immediately at hand—our breath, the knot in our stomach, the distant grind of a city garbage truck—we learn to live in the here and now. It is when we choose to dwell in our mental, abstract universe, say Buddhist teachers, that we court suffering, anxiety, and insensitivity to the needs of others. Buddhist enlightenment involves an immersion in the world rather than flight from it. By taking on the world as is, the Buddhist engages reality and at the same time no longer clings to it. His own ghosts and phantasms do not scare him; the "wide awake" Buddha is free to care for others. By choosing the here and now, the enlightened one liberates her powers of compassion.

This makes perfect sense to me as a parent. When I respond to my idea of a person, rather than the person herself, I usually create more harm for myself and for the other person than if I had just opened my eyes and noticed what was really going on. Parents can gain a foothold on spiritual liberation because they are immersed in the world of feces and mucus. They do not drift off like a helium balloon; instead they are anchored to the world by the needs and the realities of their children. By paying close attention, they accept themselves and forget themselves at the same time. Acceptance and forgetting, and self-understanding and egolessness, are all a part of spiritual enlightenment. Our children have that gift to offer. The new challenge is to extend this insight to those we encounter in the immediate family unit. Once a parent tastes what it is like to be there completely for another human being, can we begin to universalize this embrace? With friends? With our beloved work colleagues? With our most dreaded work colleagues? Can everyday parenting gain us a foothold as we climb towards greater enlightenment? If so, this would be an important insight into the spiritual element of parenting. It would become a practice, in the same way Zen meditation is a practice, to hone our powers of compassion.

6

*E*motions

A FRIEND ONCE TOLD ME THAT HAPPINESS IS SIMPLY the ability to appreciate the positive potential consequences of whatever situation we encounter. His logic was simple. "Appreciation" implies that we value something; values give our life meaning; a meaningful life is, in the end, a happy one. When our stock goes up in price, we say it appreciates in value. We can apply this fiduciary definition to our own lives—whatever we value most, we appreciate, and if we can discipline ourselves to value even the ordinary and day-to-day dimensions of life, we'll discover this appreciation. We'll see the infinite in the finite. Spiritual parents tend to be happy parents, for they appreciate the religious depths of their relationship with their children, especially when that moment of delight appears out of nowhere.

The spiritual life calls for discipline. It also calls for engagement and identification. There are times to stand back from your children, appreciate them in all of their wonder, and let them go. There are other times when you are one with them in an almost mystical union. Parents especially feel the pull of this oscillation between distance and union in their child's emotional life. Like a midwestern summer, storms of emotions gather suddenly and erupt over young children and adolescents and then disappear, leaving a seemingly refreshed and newly washed landscape.

My wife was playing tag with our six-year-old. He taunted her with a rhyme he had recently learned in the first grade. "Miss me, miss me, now you have to kiss me," he laughed. She playfully lunged for him, caught him, chuckled, and kissed him. In a second, he went from delight to despair. He began to sob, and we could not console him. Just tonight, my three-year-old mangled a "video camera" that his brother had constructed from Legos, reducing him to tears.

Like most parents, I can relate so many episodes like these as I watch my children. Outrageous emotional reactions to seemingly trivial situations punctuate the everyday lives of young children and adolescents alike. Walk into any large toy store and close your eyes. Listen. You will hear the sounds of bedlam as children wail, cry, and whine. Sounds of tormented children reverberate off the walls. In reaction, parents try everything in the book. They threaten: "I swear, Janie, if you don't stop it right now, we are leaving this store right now." Or they bargain: "Maurice, if you're good, mommy will buy you a little something. Come on, sweetie, please stop crying." Or they reason. A father reminds his daughter that they are in the store to buy a present for her cousin, and she already has too many toys, and they agreed she wouldn't get anything today, etc., etc. The children at the other end of these conversations do not back down, of course; they are not interested in reasoned debate nor are they particularly fearful of retribution. They have immediate needs and want timely satisfaction.

The emotional life of children has received enormous attention from physicians, psychologists, and philosophers. Martha Nussbaum, a classicist, philosopher, and law professor, persuasively argues that cultivating emotions is necessary to leading a moral life. In her work *Upheavals of Thought*, Nussbaum confronts the philosophical tradition that views emotion as antithetical to reason and intelligence, especially in the area of ethical theory. Many moral theorists advise us to use rationality as a guide to good moral decision-making. They argue that we should seek unerring, first principles as our ethical rudders; emotional thinking just gets in the way. Acting on our emotions, traditionally, is seen as potentially lethal as we might succumb to jealousy and rage without regard to the possible consequences of our actions. In great detail, Nussbaum rehabilitates emotions, and shows us that they help us discern value in our lives and are necessary for our ability to be compassionate and loving.

Nussbaum's research has helped me understand how much we as parents and caretakers set up a division between logic and emotion, then err on the side of reason. Test this for yourself. Take an inventory of every piece of guidance and advice you give your child in just one day. Create a chart with two categories: reason and emotion. When you tell your child to think about the consequences of his actions or to do something because it's good for him or because you are the authority, list these instructions under "reason." Guidance that acknowledges the validity of the emotional life or seeks to increase identification with happy or suffering beings should be listed under "emotion." When your child bangs into a wall and you comfort her by making her laugh (a common and quite effective technique, mind you), put that under "reason." When you comfort a crying child by letting him cry, acknowledging the reality of his pain or sadness, that's "emotion." When you laugh with your child, "emotion." When you bribe your child out of a temper tantrum, or put her in time-out for one, "reason." If you stub your toe and your toddler loans you his teddy bear for a moment of comfort and you thank her and take the bear and cuddle it, "emotion."

I will wager that, at the end of the day, the rationality column is longer than the column of emotion.

I can hear the objections to my simple system. Not all modes of rationality are equal. To throw prudence and obedience to authority into the same category is philosophically naïve. And don't we need to distinguish between good emotions and bad ones, between compassion and sheer rage? Yes, of course. My point is not that all reason is bad and all emotion good. If I believed that, I wouldn't advise you to do a two-column exercise (an analytic one) in the first place. My point is simply that we tend to ignore emotions entirely or try to suppress them, instead of thinking through what we can learn from them.

I filled out the chart one day and discovered, not surprisingly, that my rounds as a parent were overwhelmingly dedicated to imposing rationality onto my tempestuous children. Indeed, just the daily routine, including fairly strict waking, sleeping, and feeding times, creates a rational architecture for their days. In general, children's lives today are more carefully scheduled than they've been in the past, leaving less free time for imaginative play and backyard games. My sons' hockey schedules dominate our weekends. We regulate the amount of television and video and computer time. Even reading time is structured. My life as a parent and my work as a headmaster are devoted to teaching children to think ahead about the potential consequences of their decisions and actions. I've instituted and taught compulsory chess classes in my school, whose mission is to learn how to think several moves ahead. Every student in our eighth grade is required to take a class on logic and classic argumentation. The motto of the class is "you have a right to your argument, but we aren't interested in your opinions." Structure, reason, logic.

One of my worst parenting moments came when my son was six. He had been bursting into agonized tears over the slightest mishaps, like the fall of a tower of blocks or the particular spread of syrup across the surface of his pancake. When the Yankees lost, his chin would quiver and he would crumble (that's a behavior many New York grownups also exhibit, of course). So I introduced my simple algorithm of emotions and told him he could only cry over "important" things like extreme pain or the loss of a loved one. When he cried about something unimportant, I would lead him, step by step, through the logic of his decision to cry. For instance, after losing a card game, he wept. We asked him if he was in physical pain.

He answered no.

We asked him if someone he knew had died or been hurt badly.

He answered no.

We led him to the obvious conclusion that crying over a game of chance was illogical. The corollary was that he shouldn't waste tears over trivial events. How would he react when something truly awful did occur?

God bless him, he heroically tried to stop crying. He would suck in his sobs and push them back down into the pit of his stomach. But he couldn't stop. He explained to us that he understood what we were saying, that he was trying his best, but, he wailed, "I just can't stop, Daddy. You don't understand."

Why was this a case of bad, or at least ineffective, parenting? There are so many reasons. First, I was telling him that certain emotions are inappropriate to have and to express. Since my son was too young to distinguish between his emotional reaction and his self, he received the message that certain parts of him were shameful. In addition, instead of putting his mind at ease, I increased his anxiety by suggesting that tragedy inevitably lies ahead, and that we should spend our lives saving our emotional chits to spend when it strikes.

This is not to say that excessive emotion is laudable behavior. Being a bright child, my son quickly learned to put things into perspective. But he certainly didn't need me to make him into a stoic so soon in his life. Without applauding his tears, there was a gentler way to help him through his grief without being so brutally rational. I have learned that we must allow children the validity of their feelings, for they will need them to become compassionate beings and to place value on life. I have also real-

ized just how much primacy parents and our schooling institutions put on nurturing "reasonable" behavior.

Why are we such parenting rationalists? As discussed in the
chapter on "knowing," our culture is dominated by logic and technology. The human endeavor is to create order out of chaos. Crying babies spewing forth excretions certainly appear to be an
instance of this chaos. Reason is indeed a powerful tool for our survival. We use reason to solve problems and create order. It's a very
good thing to be able to ward off disease, to build bridges and
houses, to create organizational structures that maximize productivity, to fly to Mars and take pictures from the planet's surface.

In addition to seeking physical survival and economic gain, we
parents hate to see our children hurt. We spend so much time
imposing rational systems on our children mainly because we
want them to avoid physical and emotional injury as much as possible. Rationality helps us protect the young in so many obvious
ways, from avoiding toxic environments and rushing traffic and
debilitating cavities to creating strong bones and muscles and
helpful social skills. Rationality also helps us avoid sad and frightening emotions. We don't want our children to experience rage
and frustration, jealousy, and despair not only because these emotions can produce unhappy consequences but also because simply
to experience these emotions is so unpleasant. My obnoxious
directive to my son, to cry only over "important" things, was a
product of my overprotective impulses. My drive to toughen him
was inspired by my desire for him to avoid being hurt.

Balancing the need to protect our children with their need to
be themselves and to explore on their own is one of the most vex-
ing and wrenching dilemmas parents face. I have come to discover
that limiting the expression of a child's emotional life neither pro-
tects nor inures him from pain. The psychologist William Pollack
has convincingly argued that men face greater health and societal
risks such as suicide, incarceration, and early death rates because

our culture does not allow boys to enjoy an emotional life. He demonstrates that boys have just as many and as varied emotional lives as girls, but boys are afforded much narrower outlets and modes of expression. Beginning with the way we hand them off to the kindergarten teacher, telling them to be strong and not to cry, we make boys feel shameful of their normal feelings. This is such a strong and unconsciously ingrained mode of masculinity that even fathers such as I, who have the good fortune to have been enlightened by thinkers like Pollack, still teach our sons to buckle down.

~

Why are we such parenting rationalists? The human endeavor is to create order out of chaos.

~

Oscar Wilde said, "I can stand brute force, but brute reason is unbearable. There is something unfair about its use. It is hitting below the intellect." The mom or dad who sees parenting as a spiritual journey will want to meditate on Wilde's distinction between reason and intellect. Part of the religious sensibility is to be fully human with a fully integrated mind and heart. Indeed, mystical practice seeks a mode of consciousness where reason and emotions are undivided. This might be called the intellect, for we feel the world as much as we know the world. To embrace our children as thinking and feeling beings grants them authenticity and lets them be true individuals.

Does this mean that we applaud a screaming child throwing pea soup against the kitchen wall? Of course not. But there is a way to respond to this child that both accepts his anger and discourages the unacceptable expression of it. This is not a matter of technique or a turn of phrase. It is a way of being in the world, what Merton refers to as the "depth of awareness." The child who throws pea soup against the wall ought to face the consequences. He should wipe the soup off the wall or go into a time-out or at least apologize. Choose the response that fits the personality of your particular child.

At the same time, the frustration that led him to launch the bowl of soup needs to be acknowledged. I was very proud of my older son when, at the tender age of seven, he sat my wife and me down and explained that his younger brother was really annoying him and sometimes he just could not stand it, and he felt like retaliating but knew that this would only lead to more trouble. So, he asked if he could just spend a weekend away from his brother. He needed a break. In this case, he gave us the opportunity to acknowledge his frustration. Instead of punishing him for acting on his feelings, we could reward him for being so thoughtful. So after the conversation, we loaded up the car, just father and son, and headed to Cooperstown, home of the Baseball Hall of Fame. Of course, once there, he missed his little brother, and he spent his time looking for just the right gift for him.

7

Toys and Possessions

FOR THE MOST PART, THE WORLD'S RELIGIONS WARN that materialism is a barrier to spiritual enlightenment. The great sages might say that spiritual parents do not spoil their children with toys, lest they become fixated on finite concerns. This is, in general, good advice, but some aspects of prized possessions inspire the spiritual and the ethical in children and their caretakers.

The psychologist D. W. Winnicott labeled a child's teddy bear or favorite blanket or doll his or her "transitional object." The transitional object can be anything that a child uses to soothe and comfort himself. Winnicott argued that a child's transitional object marks an important step in the child's growing individuation and independence. Rather than relying on his primary caretaker for a sense of safety, the little child can turn to his bear or blanket as a representative and reminder of the fact that he is loved and nurtured and will be okay. The transitional object enables the child to move out of the home and explore new environments, such as a day-care center or pre-kindergarten. Martha Nussbaum has noted that the transitional object allows the child to develop the capacity to be alone and to feel safe at the same time, which is such an important factor in developing the imagination. In essence, the transitional object, though a concrete and tangible object, is actually an abstraction. It symbolizes the warm embrace of the child's home, internalizes it, and makes it portable.

Children keep their transitional objects long after they cease dragging them everywhere they go. At my school, we celebrate the place and importance of the transitional object in the emotional development of the children. In the fourth grade, just before students graduate to the middle school and the tumultuous world of early adolescence, we ask them to bring back to school the special "friend" they brought with them to pre-kindergarten. Every student invariably keeps these toys and blankets long after they cease clinging to them. They have been preserved in bedrooms and closets for many years and by this time are a bit ragged. I am always touched when I witness these older children, on the cusp of maturity, bringing frayed bears with missing eyes and noses to their fourth-grade classroom. This parade of fading transitional objects represents not only how much the children have grown to be strong and confident in their own right, but also how much they have been loved and nurtured, and how this care has become rooted in their internal, emotional soil.

My wife and I experienced our first sense of loss and regret as parents the night my three-year-old lost his teddy. When your baby is born, friends, family, and even business acquaintances tend to flood you with gifts, including stuffed animals and other soft, cuddly things such as blankets and hand-sewn pillows. You never know what your child will select out of this heap to be his transitional object. This is part of the mystery and power of the eventual connection. Indeed, he may pass up all the warm teddy bears and stiff giraffes and floppy frogs and choose something hard and plastic, like a toy soldier. You never know.

We were particularly blessed by the generosity of friends and colleagues when our oldest, Henry, was born. He had so many things to choose from—all soft, all colorful, all inviting intimacy and loyalty. Almost immediately, he cozied up to a red, blue, and green patchwork teddy bear from FAO Schwartz. In contrast to the plethora of stuffed animals that had been delivered to our apartment, the bear was not particularly distinguished. It was rather pedestrian as stuffed animals go. It lacked zoological verisimilitude. It was not large, and didn't talk or nod or walk. Sure, he was colorful, but other toys in his crib were even more fetching to the eye. The bear, poor bear, was nothing more than itself. But Henry loved it from the very start and soon could not be parted from it. The seeming randomness of his choice, combined with his passionate love for his bear, gave their relationship a profound and eternal quality. They were meant to be together. We called the bear "Teddy" for obvious reasons, but mostly because he represented a generic teddy bear. When Henry began to crawl, Teddy came along. When Henry could walk, Teddy accompanied him. Henry couldn't go to sleep without Teddy. Teddy went to the doctor and the supermarket and preschool. He became more than a transitional object; Teddy became a ritual as well as a member of the family.

As much as we were grateful for Teddy, he could be quite annoying. In the rush of the day, Henry would often forget him somewhere. Many nights, after a prolonged bedtime ritual that left my wife and me exhausted, Henry would realize, just as he was about to—finally—drift off to sleep, that he did not have Teddy. When it was clear that Teddy was not immediately at hand, I would turn to my wife and, in a mock PBS documentary voice, announce "once again, as night falls, the Frome family begins its nocturnal quest for Teddy." We would then launch a major search of the premises that often took on the anxious tone and scope of a Missing Persons case. Sectors of the house were divvied up among any adults who were on hand. Sometimes

Teddy was found in the yard, lying innocently by the driveway next to an overturned tricycle; other times he was tucked carelessly behind a sofa cushion.

When we travel as a family, all transitional objects come with us. Traveling with children is never relaxing, but we like to travel, and we have taken our boys with us on business and pleasure trips since they were babies. On one trip, we were spending a few days in a one-bedroom apartment in New York City visiting friends. Teddy had made the journey with us and, against our better judgment, he accompanied us on a sightseeing tour of Manhattan. Indeed, he (and we) had a very busy day. Teddy and Henry went to the zoo, played in the park, ate at a gourmet pizza parlor, visited FAO Schwartz (Teddy's ancestral home), fooled around with other toddlers, took taxis, and finally strolled home as the sun set in back of the tall buildings. We stopped at a small market to pick up dinner. Afterward, a wearied, well-dressed businessman in the elevator commented on Henry's teddy, saying that his boys never went anywhere without their bear. Henry stared at the man, hugged Teddy close to his body, and growled like a dinosaur.

By the time Henry had eaten dinner and bathed, he was exhausted. Frankly, my wife and I were looking forward to his early bedtime so we could enjoy a leisurely evening with some of our favorite take-out food. We kissed Henry goodnight; he rolled over, shut his eyes, and then rolled back again and asked, "Where's Teddy?"

And once again, as night fell, the Frome family began their nocturnal search for Teddy. The apartment was considerably smaller than our house, so it didn't take long to realize that Teddy was nowhere to be found. Henry began to sob. I don't think I've ever witnessed or heard such a raw and naked and unashamed expression of loss and remorse. Henry said that he would never be able to fall asleep again. He added that Teddy was the best friend he had ever had in the world, and he didn't know what he would do without him.

My wife and I immediately reacted according to our societally sanctioned gender roles. She sat on the edge of the bed and combed her fingers through Henry's hair trying to soothe him to sleep. I conducted a search of the building's hallways, its foyer, and the sidewalk leading up to the entrance. Then I mentally retraced every step of the day and concluded that Henry must have left Teddy in a cab. Ridiculous as this sounds, I actually called the New York City Taxi and Limousine Commission at 9 PM to report a missing blue and red and green teddy bear who was riding around in the back of a cab in one of the five boroughs. A very gentle soul took my name and number.

I told Henry that Teddy must have been left in a cab, that I had called to ask for help, and that this was the best we could do for the night. We would have to try to get some sleep and wait for a phone call in the morning. I'll never forget the anguish in my son's voice when he said, "But, Daddy, you don't understand. Teddy needs me. He's going to be so alone in the back of the taxi. He is going to be so sad. He won't be able to make it without me."

We tried to calm him by making up a happy story about Teddy's cab ride all over New York City. "I bet he's gazing at the Brooklyn Bridge right now and yelling at the cabbie to take him to the Empire State Building."

"No, he's crying; he's not having fun. He's crying; I know it." Henry would have none of our optimism.

"How do you know he's crying?"

"Because I'm crying," Henry responded, his logic immediately silencing us.

He finally fell asleep. My wife and I had lost our appetite for take-out food and we just went to bed. My wife started to cry. She explained that even though she knew Teddy was just a toy, something about Henry's attachment to him was real and deep and deserving of respect. I had to admit that even I, a practicing pragmatist, felt a wrenching sadness in my soul. My mind began to fill with images of Teddy on the muddy floor of a cab zooming over the Brooklyn Bridge. Perhaps the driver had just picked up a bunch of snotty yuppies pouring out of a trendy nightclub; they wouldn't even notice Teddy as their designer shoe toes carelessly poked him under the driver's seat. Once lodged there, no one might notice Teddy until the cab was thoroughly vacuumed and cleaned. And when would that occur? Perhaps never. The cabs I rode in were always grimy.

The chances of ever retrieving Teddy began to fade. Suddenly, I bolted upright in bed. I realized (as you probably already have realized) that Teddy had to be in the apartment because I remembered our elevator ride with the tired businessman. His comment about Teddy was made just before dinner, and Henry hadn't left the building since. Teddy must have been somewhere between the elevator doors and our apartment. I shook my wife awake. We turned on all of the lights and searched the apartment from top to bottom all over again. Then I remembered that Henry was at the stage where he liked to hide things in nooks and crannies. We looked behind every chair and couch and lamp. I rifled through the desk. We emptied the dresser in the living room and there, in the third drawer, we found Teddy, neatly laid to rest. We could not wait for the morning to come. We woke Henry up and reunited him with his bear. Henry smiled, pulled Teddy tightly to his chest, and rolled back to sleep.

I found it remarkable that we had internalized our son's grief over the loss of a stuffed animal that we could have replaced the next day. In fact, after this incident, we did buy two more of the identical brand of bear, but Henry could always tell the difference between the original Teddy and his understudies. It might have been a psychic or a fragrant connection, but the original Teddy would always enjoy the level of wear-and-tear and worn-down softness that made him easily distinguished. I've always marveled that this kind of profound connection could be made at such a young age. The beloved is that which is the most threadbare, and the beloved's shabbiness results from days and nights of holding on for dear life. The more Teddy's skin pilled, the more his arms drooped off his shoulders as if they had been dislocated, the more organs he lost (like his button eyes) the more his nose disappeared until it became a ragged hole—the more Henry loved him. Indeed, Teddy eventually resembled a leper, and yet his state of disrepair was exactly what marked him as the one—indeed, the one and only one.

~

Even though Teddy was just a toy, something about Henry's attachment to him was real and deep and deserving of respect.

~

I'm not arguing that love wears the beloved out, though in a more cynical mood, I might say something along those lines. It's wonderful that the intense passion for the transitional object helps the child understand a kind of love that approaches a deep spiritual bond. The Greeks distinguished at least three kinds of love: *eros*, or physical love; *philos*, or the act of loving something like wisdom or mankind; and *agape*, or spiritual love. In the early Christian church, *agape* was the kind of love associated with the Eucharist. *Agape* is eternal; *agape* transcends physical deterioration; *agape* is pure and unchanging. The bond a child has with his or her transitional object approaches *agape*. Our fourth-grade parade of transitional objects demonstrates that the children's love for their blankets and bears was not based on temporal beauty or perfection. This was a love for the ages.

The goal is, of course, for the child to be able to transfer these feelings of *agape* to real, human relationships. Buddhism teaches that attachment to things and to our own needy emotions gives rise to suffering. To practice nonattachment is to begin to release one's self from the cycle of pain. If we do not cling to our petty needs, we are free to help others. Nonattachment, in Buddhist practice, increases our powers of compassion. On the other hand, I think the child's clinging relationship with his transitional object is a lesson in the religious value of certain modes of attachment.

Psychologists theorize that the transitional object helps the child make the transition to independence away from his original caregivers. The transitional object also gives your child his or her first lesson in pure, spiritual love, connection, and compassion. It teaches your child to care. It teaches your children to climb out of their developmentally appropriate egocentrism, giving them, for the first time, a sense of the needs of another. When your daughter puts pajamas on her pony and tucks him in for the night, she is practicing compassion in an important way. In a few years, the pony's legs will dangle from its body by a few thin threads, and your daughter's love will only grow. Our goal as parents and educators must be to try to seize on young children's natural loving loyalty, this feeling of *agape* that transcends and outlasts physical deterioration, and encourage children to hold on to it as they mature into adolescence and begin to swim in a culture obsessed with transient beauty. Keep those ragged bears and blankets in your child's room as a memento and a reminder of a time when, effortlessly and naturally, they radiated spiritual wisdom.

8

_D_iscipline

So far, I have highlighted humility, compassion, and reverence for the mystery of the universe as characteristics of the religious impulse. My fundamental view is that these same qualities can also be found in the parenting experience. Parenting can be considered an avenue of and for spiritual experience. There are, of course, other avenues. There are also other religious dimensions besides humility, compassion, and reverence. One of these is the concept of sin or a sense of having fallen away from the truth or the light. As we walk the path of parenting, we will experience the light and we will see the darkness. As it is important to fully appreciate the positive dimensions of what children bring to our lives, it is equally important to recognize the spiritually potent aspects of those times when parents and children fall away from each other and themselves.

This is a difficult chapter to write because the idea of sin is complicated and invites so many different interpretations. If we take a short walk through some of the world's most representative religions, we will find a great variety of ideas on what it means to be fallen.

Islamic theology defines a sinner as anyone who refuses to follow the path of Allah. Islam literally means "submission," and the basic tenet of Islam is to submit to the will of Allah. On the day of reckoning, your transgressions will be tallied, and you will be held accountable. The opening of the scripture in the Qur'an states:

> In the name of Allah, the Beneficent, the Merciful,
> 1. Praise be to Allah, Lord of the Worlds,
> 2. The Beneficent, the Merciful,
> 3. Owner of the Day of Judgment.
> 4. Thee (alone) we worship; Thee (alone) we ask for help.
> 5. Show us the straight path,
> 6. The path of those whom Thou hast favored;
> 7. Not (the path) of those who earn Thine anger nor of those who go astray.

In Christianity and Judaism, as well, people believe that God's instructions are central to leading the religious life. There are over six hundred commandments in the Hebrew Bible alone. To sin is to stray from God's tenets. Christian and Jewish ideas of sin are combined in the following passage from John's First Epistle:

> My children, I am writing this to you so that you should not commit sin. But if anybody does, we have in Jesus Christ one who is acceptable to God and will plead our cause with the Father. He is himself a sacrifice to atone for our sins, and not ours only but the sins of the whole world. It is by keeping God's commandments that we can be sure we know him. Whoever says "I know him," but does not obey his commands, is a liar and the truth is not in him; but whoever is obedient to his word, in him the love of God is truly made perfect. This is how we can be sure that we are in him. (2:1–5)

The three great monotheistic religions agree that our duty is to love God and to obey God. Sin is therefore a matter of not following certain rules and, at the same time, not cultivating a certain kind of relationship with God. Judaism, Christianity, and Islam may differ on the nature of God and God's exact prescriptions for human behavior, but they do agree that we have a duty to supplicate ourselves freely and joyfully to the will and being of God.

Eastern religions have a very different notion of man's fallen state. It would indeed be misleading to label this an idea of sin at all. Hinduism, Buddhism, and Taoism, for instance, take a more philosophical and psychological approach when they describe the roots of human suffering. In these religious traditions, it is not a matter of being obedient to a set of rules or entering into a relationship with a divinity. In Eastern spirituality, we stray from the path of enlightenment when we fail to understand that our common perceptions of the world are distorted illusions and that the universe is not divided into this and that, good and bad, right and wrong, you and me, my country and your country. Rather, Eastern religions strive to view the really real as holistic or radically all-inclusive.

This idea of rising above opposites and seeking peace in oneness is clearly stated in the Mundaka Upanishad from the Hindu scriptures:

When the wise seer beholds in golden glory the Lord, the Spirit, the Creator of the god of creation, then he leaves good and evil behind and in purity he goes to the unity supreme.

And Taoism, as in this passage from chapter 81 in the *Tao Tê Ching*:

True Words are not fine-sounding;
Fine sounding words are not true.
The good man does not prove by argument;
And he who proves by argument is not good.
True wisdom is different from much learning;

Much learning means little wisdom . . .
For Heaven's way is to sharpen without cutting,
And the Sage's way is to act without striving.

Eastern religions are more interested in creating an egoless way
of being rather than discovering a set of rules. As the Tibetan Buddhist master Chögyam Trungpa explains, the enlightened person
(the bodhisattva) doesn't need a finite set of moral precepts; she
always acts well because she always acts out of a root of love and
compassion: "For if a bodhisattva is completely selfless, a completely open person, then he will act according to openness, will
not have to follow rules; he will simply fall into patterns. It is
impossible for the bodhisattva to destroy or harm other people,
because he embodies transcendental generosity."

Both Eastern and Western religions agree, I think, that sin or
fallenness or suffering or being unenlightened involve some kind
of alienation from the ultimate reality, the Source, as it were, of
what is truly real and sacred. I am assuming that none of us are
saints or bodhisattvas. As parents, we will transgress the dictates
of conduct found in the Hebrew Bible, the New Testament and
the Qu'ran. We will many times fail to love God. We will be alienated from our Creator. We will drift away from our best and most
compassionate selves. We will see the world as fractured and divi-
sive. We will operate from a self-centered orientation. We will be
at war with our lives and retreat back to an "us versus them" and
a "me versus him (or her)" mental encampment. Depending on
your religious background, as a parent, you will either sin or your
spiritual ignorance and limitation will cause you and those you
encounter much suffering.

And so will your children. There are things that your children
will do and say, whether they are two or twenty-two, that will horrify you. They will naturally break most of the commandments.
At some point they will lie; they will not honor you; they will
covet a lot, especially if they watch children's television, shop at a

toy store, or visit the house of a more affluent friend. The vast majority will not kill, but they may clobber their sibling over the head with a plastic hammer for no apparent reason; they will "borrow" without asking; they may swear at inopportune times. Your children will also demonstrate, from time to time, their alienation from the divine source and show a profoundly egocentric way of being, thus wandering from both the Eastern and monotheistic spiritual paths. They will not share. They will hurt the feelings of their friends and peers. They will fail to consider your needs. They will hate with an unbelievable fury. Your toddler or your adolescent may throw wild temper tantrums, flailing about your living room. They may seek to destroy their bodies

~

Your children will naturally break most of the commandments. At some point they will lie; they will not honor you; they will covet a lot.

~

with drugs, binges of alcohol, irresponsible sex, or extravagant piercing. They may suddenly withdraw deeply into themselves and stop bathing or talking or going to school—or doing much of anything at all. They may escape their bedrooms at night, tightly bundled in a hooded sweatshirt, to wander the worst parts of your city or town.

These are some of the innumerable ways that I, as a parent and as an educator, have witnessed our children's alienation from harmony and divinity. Like on any spiritual path you hike, both the sublime and the terrifying will emerge, and both will appear unexpectedly. I once taught a ninth grader named Ian. Ian was a beautiful young boy, impeccably dressed in a blue blazer, rep tie, and striped, cotton, button-down shirt. Ian lived with his father and his sister. No one ever mentioned his mother; her absence would always remain a mystery. Due to his father's work, Ian had lived all over the world. His divergent experiences gave him a more mature, cosmopolitan, and somewhat sad air. He was quiet and thoughtful, and we quickly struck up a relationship. The other boys did not dislike him, but neither did they cozy up to him. Ian preferred the company of adults.

As the school year began, I sized Ian up as a potential intellectual who enjoyed poetry and history. I looked forward to watching him grow over his four years of upper school. When the mid-semester grades came out, Ian was doing miserably. While not failing, he was struggling with Cs. We knew from his admissions testing that he possessed the intelligence to keep up with the work. His father quickly came to Ian's rescue and told the school that it was our fault. We had not adequately structured his schedule and his day to ensure Ian's success. When Ian and I spoke, Ian suggested that he was bored. This confirmed my initial estimation that he was a romantic poet tethered in a preppie straightjacket. I delivered long monologues to Ian about how academic skills can actually liberate one's self by cultivating powerful tools for self-expression. Ian listened politely, but rarely responded except to say that he promised to do better.

As the semester wore on, Ian slipped into more and more of a catatonic funk. He stopped doing homework altogether; he refused to participate in school activities; he stopped talking. Ian would dutifully show up to school on time, always impeccably dressed. He would give us nothing more. Ian began to remind me of Melville's character Bartelby the Scrivener, who shows up for work but refuses to perform any tasks, stating politely but firmly "I would prefer not to."

As he began to fail all of his subjects, his teachers grew more irate. They interpreted his inactivity as belligerence and disrespect. I decided to "save" Ian, figuring that I was the only one who could understand him. I tried being his confederate, stating that I too felt the absurdity of the game of school, but that it was one that was worthwhile to play in the long run. Ian would just stare at me. As I reflect on Ian, it occurs to me that he had never once told me why he'd stopped working. I had assumed it was for existential reasons, but he never talked about absurdity or conformity. Those were my words. When being his buddy failed to work, I switched tactics and became punitive. I threatened expulsion. I kept him after school. I conducted numerous conferences with his father. We suggested therapy. It turned out he had been in therapy for years, even before he came to the school. The psychiatrist prescribed Ritalin, thinking that Ian might have attention deficit disorder. Nothing worked. I remember, near the end, looking into Ian's eyes and seeing no life at all. I thought that Ian's soul had left him.

When we finally had to tell Ian that we could no longer keep him at the school, he shrugged and left my office to clean out his locker. His father stayed behind and told me that Ian was full of hate. Ian had reported having an out-of-body experience on the Ritalin. One night, as he watched a basketball game, he watched himself watching the television. This had only served to further alienate his son. His father said: "He hates everyone—me, his sister, this school, and especially you, Mr. Frome."

I saw Ian again a few years later. My wife and I were coming out of a restaurant in a marginal neighborhood. We saw four boys in baggy trousers and hooded sweatshirts across the street in a vacant lot. They were glowering at us and we got the feeling they were considering some sort of mugging. We quickly got in a cab. I looked out the window at the boys and recognized Ian's pale, still angelic face under one of the hoods. He stared back, empty of expression. He seemed to be beyond hate.

Ian had clearly suffered a psychic wound that was unfathomable to everyone who cared about him. He was beyond our reach. I always had the feeling that some force had grabbed him by the ankle and was constantly dragging him back into the darkness. At the same time, the adults in his life could never climb out of their own egocentric view of Ian and what Ian should be and do. I was guilty of romanticizing Ian. He was not a poetic soul, a Keatsian character, but a little boy bewildered and angry. It makes sense that he hated me. From his point of view, I was so repulsed by his actual state of being that I recast him as a fictional character. His psychiatrist reduced his psychic suffering to a physical disease and alienated him from the one thing he might call his own, namely his pain, by drugging him. His father refused to respect Ian as someone who was strong enough to be held responsible for the consequences of his actions. By always blaming the school, his father infantilized Ian, humiliating the fourteen-year-old boy and further enraging him. In the end, no one was honest; no one spoke plainly; no one just stated what was the case; no one was objective. We were all ensnared by the limitations of our own selves and did little to save him—if indeed anything could have saved him.

I think of the Buddha's "Fire Sermon" when I reflect on Ian.

Monks, the All is aflame. What All is aflame? The eye is aflame. Forms are aflame. Consciousness at the eye is aflame. Contact at the eye is aflame. And whatever there is that arises in dependence on contact at the eye—experienced as pleasure, pain, or neither-pleasure-nor-pain—that too is aflame. Aflame with what? Aflame with the fire of passion, the fire of aversion, the fire of delusion. Aflame, I tell you, with birth, aging, and death, with sorrows, lamentations, pains, distresses, and despairs.

All of the adults who dealt with Ian were on fire in the blaze of their own ego. Ian himself was so blinded by the contours of his pain, he could only see the hands reaching out to him as serpents intent on biting him.

Both the monotheistic and Eastern traditions regard selfishness and self-centeredness as the roots of evil or sin or the unenlightened state. Instead of God or the good of humanity, the sinner elevates his ego to be the ultimate concern. In so doing, the fallen ones divide and fracture the universe. As Henri Nouwen has pointed out, the word "diabolic" means to divide. Nouwen argued that when we experience the unified, undivided reality of the universe, when we see life and death and success and failure as part of the same force, we are truly close to God.

Parenting is a spiritual experience because it forces you out of yourself. Becoming a parent is often the first experience young adults have with being there totally for an other. Parenting also tends to make one more in tune with the rhythm of life. At its best, it helps us overcome our own alienation. Yet parenting can and will often highlight our fallen and unenlightened state. A spiritual theory of parenting would be incomplete and false if it did not acknowledge the importance of sin, however you define it, as part of the religious experience you can have with children. When your child makes a mistake, it is crucial that they be held accountable as part of their journey away from egocentricism. We will talk more about the difference between love and indulgence in another chapter. Nevertheless, the adults in a child's life must also move out of their own circle of ego and see themselves and their children in as objective a way as possible. To discipline outside of the demands of the self is compassionate and spiritually liberating. To discipline, as we all did with Ian, from the compass point of our own ego, is to foment the cycle of sin and alienation. If parenting is to be regarded as a form of spiritual practice, it must be then a constant journey away from our selves toward a more holistic, unified experience of the universe as we move toward atonement and peace.

9

*D*oubling:
On They Being You

WE'VE JUST DISCUSSED HOW THE NATURE OF SIN INFORMS
how you might discipline your child. In discussing sin or evil as
expressed in some of the world's religions, I neglected to mention
concepts of hell or eternal punishment for unredeemed sin. In
many religious traditions, your actual punishment is to have to
live with the self that you've created. Satan's humanist heresy in
Milton's *Paradise Lost*, "The mind is its own place, and in
itself/Can make a heav'n of hell, a hell of heav'n," is shared by a
number of religious thinkers, including Stoic philosophers and
the mystic Jakob Boehme. Boehme took Jesus's teaching that "the
kingdom of God is within you" to mean that heaven and hell are
individual states of mind. The Qu'ran's vivid depictions of the
pleasures of heaven and the pains of hell imply that the individual is ultimately responsible for the state of his or her own soul;
after death, you are left to suffer or delight in the soul you have
created. This sentiment is echoed in *The Tibetan Book of the Dead*.
"During the journey after death, the loved one is confronted with
a series of tantalizing lights. One is soft and blue and particularly
inviting, but it is only your unconscious tendencies, accumulated

by your intense pride." To choose this light, that is to choose your self after physical death—means to be reborn again to the cycle of suffering and death.

Children are neither heaven nor hell, but they do reflect us back on our selves, showing us the best, worst, and unacknowledged parts of our being. Like the variety of bright lights that flash before the departed in *The Tibetan Book of the Dead*, they can liberate us by distracting us from our egos, or they can condemn us by driving us further into ourselves. In the end, if we pay close attention, they show us to ourselves in ways we have never experienced.

Be careful of the soul and the patterns of behavior you cultivate before you have children, for they will come back to live with you, to taunt you, to haunt you in the guise of your sons and daughters. For instance, my sons now loudly sing silly songs in the morning as they get ready for school. These mock songs only add to the sense of chaos. Indeed, they are quite annoying. When I once lost my patience and told both of them to knock off the singing, they looked at me blankly and said "But, Dad, you sing songs every morning." They were right. I do have a dumb habit of putting idiotic words to standard melodies as I shave and dress. I'd never noticed this before my sons began to mirror my behavior.

On the other hand, you need to forgive yourself for your personality deficits so that when your child exhibits them you do not punish her in order to flagellate yourself. I once had a close friend, Kurt, a wonderful, talented, loving man who never found a center to his life and so was unable to enjoy the fruits of his love and work. His mother spent much of her time away from the home in spiritual retreats or mental hospitals. He lived with his father. Kurt told me that when he was a boy, his father would scold him whenever he acted like his father. This was not an unconscious impulse on the part of his father. It was a deliberate, articulated family policy that whenever Kurt acted in a way that resembled his father, he would be upbraided.

Kurt's father was a deeply talented abstract painter, but also a tortured soul who loathed himself. I've met him a few times. You can see the source of many of Kurt's fine qualities in his father: his energy, his humor, his intellectual hunger, his questioning spirit, his creativity, his ability to tell a story and to entertain friends. Kurt tells me, though, that whenever he exercised any of these attributes, his father would literally sit him down and say: "You are beginning to act like me; you don't want to act like me; I want you to be different so you don't have to suffer like I do." As the years passed, Kurt's father stopped explaining, and just reacted whenever Kurt resembled him.

Kurt told me a story that when he was about eight, a salesman visited the house. The man spent some time with his parents and as he was leaving Kurt came to the door and said "Don't call us, we'll call you." Kurt says that he knew the guy was trying to sell something, and he was trying to make light of the situation. As the salesman walked away, Kurt's father, enraged, knocked Kurt to the floor, and said, "Don't ever try to be funny."

As an adult, Kurt can admit that in that situation he was inappropriate and probably deserved a lesson in manners. On the other hand, his father was famous for his cutting wit, and Kurt was trying some of it out on his own. It is his father's fury, though, that has stuck with Kurt all of these years. I have suggested to Kurt that his father was really knocking himself down, despondent that he'd created another version of his self doomed to wander the world feeling alone, rootless, and unaccepted.

Ironically, despite his best effort, his father nurtured a similar soul in his son. They were both rootless, unmoored, and difficult. Kurt looked like a healthy, well-adjusted guy. Indeed, he was quite popular and always had lots of girlfriends. But, he once confided in me, he never felt at home with himself or with the world. At a wedding once, a drunken psychologist I knew stumbled into Kurt and said, "You just aren't comfortable in your own skin, are you?"

We laughed about this for years, teasing him that she had come so close to the truth about him after only a few glasses of champagne.

Kurt looked for a sense of self in religion, possessions, fashion, writers, travel, sports, art, women—anything, that is, that might give him validation and a foothold in the world. But the more validation Kurt received, the lonelier and more disconnected he felt. When people began to like him, he soon rejected their friendship or intimacy. And if he got good at something or received positive feedback, he would likely quit. Kurt once wrote the first three chapters of a novel. He attended an open mike at a coffeehouse and read his work. The audience loved his work. They laughed at all the right places and seemed genuinely engaged in the story. At the end of the reading, a writing professor from the University of Virginia approached Kurt and told him how much he loved his writing. He encouraged him to get his MFA and to use his novel-in-progress as his thesis. Kurt stopped writing the next day.

As soon as a woman got close to him, he would distance himself. He did this to his friends as well. In fact, Kurt and I drifted apart after he revealed just how much personal pain he carried with him. I remember sitting in one of the old dining halls at our university. It was early spring and the rotunda of the hall looked out on budding forsythia and a cloudless blue sky. Kurt remarked how beautiful the setting was and how much it hurt him that he just could not enjoy it. He had lost the ability to relish everyday life. I marveled at how a person who had so much—talent, good looks, friends, intelligence—was so lost in the world. Kurt seemed to peer out on life from the cage of his mind. Occasionally, he would extend his hands through its bars and try to touch someone else, but his grasp was not long enough. Indeed, he told me once that when he was a boy he read the Classics Illustrated version of Mary Shelley's *Frankenstein*. The last frame of the cartoon showed an image of the monster alone and adrift on an iceberg. Kurt said he could never remove that picture, garishly colored in blue and purple and black and white, from his mind. Even when he became a young man, it remained vividly etched in his consciousness as a symbol for himself.

What became of Kurt, I don't know, though I've heard he settled down to raise a family, becoming a pillar of his community. In any case, Kurt's story is an important one for the spiritual parent. Milton's Satan argues that it is not for God to punish us; the creative powers of the mind can find meaning and beauty in the most horrid of conditions, and we can also make our blessings into instruments of torture. A parent who has not done enough soul work and introspection often creates a living spiritual hell for his children even though he may dwell in a veritable paradise. Kurt grew up on a secluded estate in the hills, next to a brook. He wandered in fields and pear orchards; famous musicians and artists were frequent guests. Kurt's recollection of his boyhood was one long summer evening with music and jugs of wine and long tables laden with food in the back yard. In many ways, it was what would seem an idyllic childhood. Yet his parents were haunted by their own hells and imposed them, however unconsciously, on their son. Despite the lyrical appearance of the home, Kurt was relegated to a life of numbed alienation. Dwelling in the charged and fragile emotional atmosphere his parents created, Kurt's only chance for survival was to withdraw from himself and from others. Kurt's withdrawal though was no escape. It just dug out another ring in his personal hell.

A central part of the spirituality of parenting is the unpredictability of raising children. Science and reason are tools we use to lessen the impact of chance on our lives. Theology and spirituality are pursuits we engage in to come to terms with the tremendous mystery that eludes the calipers of logic and scientific experimentation. The spiritual parent does not ignore reason, but, at the same time, she remains open to the humbling uncertainty and radical freedom of her children. When we walk the spiritual path, we must expect joy and sorrow, redemption and trial, revelation and confusion. By raising the issue of hell in parenting, I am not entirely taking the side of Milton's Satan. He believes that we can control for heaven and hell; we just must make up our minds. If Milton's Satan were a little more modern, I think he would say that with some good therapy we could make a heaven of hell. He might even recommend a pharmacological solution.

~

The spiritual parent does not ignore reason, but she remains open to the humbling uncertainty and radical freedom of her children.

~

I am arguing something more ambiguous. Some parents believe that they can create a perfect environment for their children. As I mentioned in the first chapter, parents go to great lengths to ensure that their children have everything in their environment firmly in place to maximize their full potential. But one of these environmental factors is your own mental health. I know many families who hire, along with the SAT coach and private tutor, the best therapist in town to cleanse them of their neurotic tendencies. A good therapist is a blessed partner in becoming and being a parent, but seeking to rid yourself of your negative parts in order to create a heavenly soil for your child is a symptom of the drive to control and dominate. Effective and long-lasting therapy is not a purging exercise, but a part of a life-long exploration of the self. It is never over and done with. Just like your children, you are a riddle that will never be solved.

We must accept ourselves as limited and expect ourselves to be limited. Then, after much personal reflection and sincere work, we must seek to mitigate the most destructive effects that our unconscious may have on our children. Still, our residue will stick to them; when it does, we need to offer our hand to them to get them out of the ruts we have dug for them. This hand must extend from the same generous spirit we extend to ourselves as well.

We will all do things and say things to our children that hurt them and arise out of deeply seeded, unresolved conflicts we have with our own parents. This cannot be avoided. I find extended family gatherings rather tedious. I know this about myself, and yet sometimes I find it hard not to express my frustration when yet another seemingly trivial extended family function imposes itself on my time. What a terrible role model I must be for my two sons who will go off and form their own families and create, by definition, more extended family functions. I know this about myself, and yet I cannot quite stop myself to create a heaven of hell the next time I am forced to go to some third-cousin-once-removed's wedding. I fight to stop myself, but I know that I will never purify myself of these emotions. At the same time, once my kids were old enough, I told them why I felt the way I did. I told them I was wrong. I told them that it was my responsibility to overcome this unconscious tendency. I apologized for making things hard. But I did not expect a quick solution. I could vow to struggle against the walls of the hell that I was helping to create. I could also vow to keep my own children out of my cell by recognizing the very cell within which I dwelt.

The theme of this chapter is more than the old saying that the sins of the father will be visited upon his sons. That is too causal and too formulaic to reflect the mystery of parenting. Jesus's parable of seeds and soils in Matthew 13:3–8 gets closer to what I want to say. Jesus explains that a farmer can sow many seeds on many types of terrain. The birds eat some seeds; others fall on rocky soil, grow quickly, and get burned by the sun. Thorns kill some of the other seeds, but some do fall on good soil and bring forth a harvest. Yet, still, the bounty of the harvest is unpredictable: "Other seeds fell on good soil and brought forth grain, some a hundredfold, some sixty, some thirty."

This parable can be interpreted from a number of different perspectives. It speaks to parents, though, of the tenuous nature of our influence on our children. We all know terrific mothers and fathers who have difficult, amoral children. We are also familiar with responsible, loving adults who came from dysfunctional, unhappy homes. I think it too simplistic to equate the seeds in the parable with parents and the soil to our children. Jesus's story is about the delicate interaction between seed and soil; that is, it addresses growth or decay as a byproduct of parental influence and how it is received and internalized by our children. As parents, we are responsible for the environment within which our children grow. But children are also responsible for how they make meaning of their inherited environment. In other words, Jesus circumvents a simple "if I do this, then that will happen" causal view of parenting. It is much more complex than that. Sometimes the vagaries of accident disrupt this relationship when the birds of fate swoop down upon a perfectly fertile path and gobble up the seeds. On other occasions, it is our own carelessness or ignorance that breeds disaster when we plant seeds on rocks and thorns. But even the best relationship between seed and soil yields unpredictable results. Growth is sometimes modest in the best of circumstances; sometimes it is wildly robust.

As parents, we are continually helping to creating conditions of heaven and conditions of hell for and with our children. There is no way of predicting the results of our sowing. Parenting is not about results; it is about children. Children may result from our parenting, but to call them results is to rob them of their freedom and humanity and to ignore that it is the relationship between soil and seed that is the most important factor. Authentic, spiritual parenting calls us to be as self-aware as possible of our own personal tendencies and habits. Our children will reflect the worst and the best parts of ourselves, forcing us to take a good, long objective look at ourselves. A friend of mine told me that his daughter is just as stubborn as he is. Then he added, "Only worse!" My friend's perception that she is more stubborn than her father is a matter of the power of the mirror she is holding up to him. She is refracting him to himself, and in so doing, she is forcing her father to climb out of the blindness his egocentricity has created. Recognizing yourself in your children can be painful, but it allows you to grow too. It allows you to detach yourself from illusions about yourself that you may have clung to for most of your life. In this way, parenting, if you open yourself to all of its joyous and painful implications, can spiritually liberate you—dare I say, even redeem you? Perhaps. But only if, in the spirit of sincere seekers of truth in all of the faith traditions, you pay full attention to the often painful possibilities of redemption.

We need to continually seek to understand the systemic implications of the way our children react to us and to the home culture we have unconsciously created. We should certainly be careful of rocks and thorns and scorching sun. But when our seeds do land in those kinds of places, we need to stay with them, kneel before them on this dry bit of ground and nurture them as much as we can. Look out for the birds and try to weed out a patch of good soil. Even then, you will never be sure of the extent of your seed's growth. Beware, the seed may show you to yourself in surprising and shocking ways. As William Sloane Coffin reminds us, St. Augustine once said, "Never fight evil as if it were something that arose totally outside of yourself." Your children may become you, only worse. In this case, forgive yourself then lose yourself, and truly begin to love them.

10

$\mathcal{R}$ituals

EVERY FAMILY WITH CHILDREN STILL LIVING AT HOME engages in daily tasks. Each day you wake with your children, you eat with your children or at least feed them, and you put them down to sleep. Depending on their age, you may also clothe them, bathe them, and drive them somewhere—to school or a lesson or a sports practice. Frankly, these tasks can be annoying and exhausting. But when we learn to see these rounds as rituals rather than chores, we can begin to recognize the spiritual opportunities of parenting. We begin to recognize the daily hierophanies that life with children presents.

What's the difference between a chore and a ritual? Chores are routine jobs that we perform in order to accomplish a concrete objective. We tend to do them and move on to something else. Chores focus on the product; rituals focus on the process. A ritual usually involves a community following a prescribed practice or routine. Rituals rarely, in and of themselves, produce a tangible, immediate, concrete result. When a ritual is meaningful it points beyond itself to an important, fundamental shared truth. In other words, rituals, though they involve tasks, are also symbolic of something more than the mere activity of the ritual. Rituals lose meaning when they are performed like a chore. We see this in church services. When communion becomes merely eating, drinking, and a signal that the church service is about to be over (so it's time to gather your coat and prepare to leave in order to beat the crowd), its religious significance shrivels and dies. The parent who seeks a spiritual understanding of her role will try to see daily routines such as eating, sleeping, waking, and clothing as meaningful rituals involving a communion of souls.

This is easier said than done. If I honestly look at my family's daily "rituals," they resemble anything but a communion with the eternal. In the morning, my wife leaves at 6:45 AM for her hour-long commute. I stomp down the stairs while my older son, Henry, wakes up and dresses himself. He usually crawls into our bed and turns on the television. I stand at the bottom of the stairs and ask him what he would like for breakfast. Henry does not respond. I hear the drone of ESPN SportsCenter. I raise my voice and ask whether he's dressed or not. Still no response, except I have now awakened his younger brother, Spencer, who realizes that his mother has already left for work without giving him a goodbye hug. Spencer starts to cry. I retreat back into the kitchen and fry an egg for myself, then backtrack to the foot of the stairs armed now with threats.

"Henry, if you don't come down here this minute I'm leaving without you."

Henry finally responds with "Okay, Dad, I'm sorry, I didn't hear you." He trots down the stairs with his little brother in tow inevitably screaming, "Henry, it's not a race." Henry calmly responds, "I know, I know, I just happened to be first." This of course makes Spencer cry, for he desperately wants to beat his big brother at something.

In order for us to get to school on time, we now have barely ten minutes to eat, brush our teeth, and load up the car. Henry deliberates on his cereal choice as I watch the minutes tick by. Our nanny, Janelle, arrives, which is some relief for Spencer, but Henry continues to dawdle over the right amount of milk in his bowl. In his mind, too much will make the cereal inedible, but too little is also unacceptable. I trudge back up the stairs making idle threats, brush my teeth, and grab my jacket. When I come back, Henry has suddenly decided to write and illustrate a new story. He is in the family room collecting paper and asking for a green pen. Janelle gets involved, coaching him to brush his teeth and put his coat on. Henry runs to the bathroom as I go out to car. He pleads with me not to leave without him. Janelle now barks orders—get your backpack, get your coat, that coat's not warm enough, Daddy is going to leave without you, etc. In a mad dash, Henry explodes out the front door and climbs into the backseat. I close his door and back out of the driveway pontificating that we have got to get out of the house on time from now on, which leads to a sermon on work and then an explanation of how I need to work to provide Henry with all the things he enjoys in life, like his home and his school and his toys, and how his making me late jeopardizes all of that. Henry sits in silence.

In my household this routine occurs on almost every weekday morning. I do not recommend it to anyone, and I know that I commit several fundamental parenting errors each morning from delivering idle threats to overly abstract sermonizing.

How can this stressful chaos reveal anything spiritual or holy or even slightly meaningful? One morning, I absolutely had to be at work by a specific time. Henry dawdled as usual, and Janelle (who is going to be a great mother when she has kids) whispered that I should just leave. She would take Henry to school, finally teaching him that there were consequences to his actions. I yelled up to Henry that this time I was serious, and I was leaving that instant. I left the house and backed the car up slowly, hoping he would burst out of the house at the last minute. He didn't, and I drove away. Despite the ease of not having to drive my son to school, and despite the certainty I'd make it on time to my "crucial" appointment, my stomach sank. I wanted to cry. Every day, without complaint or fuss, Henry and I do happily drive to work together and listen to music. Though the prelude of dressing and breakfasting is filled with stress and tension, we are settled once we enter the car. We don't talk much; we just *are* together, wordlessly. On that morning, I finally realized how much I love and need this ritual with my son, and how meaningful it is to me. In the isolation of the car and through the sharing of something we both love—music—Henry and I find our connection. Commuting to work each morning is not a chore, but a meaningful ritual.

When I returned home that evening, Janelle told me that Henry had been devastated when he realized I'd left for my meeting without him. He wept and said over and over again, "I never have any time with my Daddy." She said that it broke her heart and that she tried to explain to him that it was *he* who had chosen to take too much time, so he could only blame himself. Henry, being only six, may have understood this on some level. More profoundly, though, he felt lost without his morning drive, the same way a truly faithful Catholic must feel when she misses mass, or a Buddhist when she skips meditation practice. Henry's morning ritual in the car is more than a drive; it's one of the ways he grounds himself in a chaotic world. We both discovered that our commute had become a serious, spiritual ritual.

Because it is by definition more calming than the morning routine, the ritual of bedtime lends itself more readily to spiritual reflection. All families that I know of deliberately practice different bedtime rituals. As soon as we become parents, we begin to choreograph how we put our child to sleep. Some families take a long, hot bath. Others pray, or have a chat about the events of the day. Almost all parents read to their children at this time. Educators recommend bedtime stories as the best way to introduce our children to the pleasures and comforts of reading. But we don't do this just because of the child-rearing experts. In fact, even before they had children, many adults put themselves to bed by reading. Sleep and reading seem to go hand and hand. Think about how many novels open with the main character either just waking up or just falling to sleep. Marcel Proust's masterpiece, *In Search of Lost Time*, for example, opens with the narrator first falling asleep and then waking up again.

∼

He felt lost without his morning drive, the same way a truly faithful Catholic must feel when she misses mass, or a Buddhist when she skips meditation practice.

∼

Just what is it about going to sleep that recommends reading? Rabbi Nancy Fuchs notes that sleep is a mysterious dimension wherein our mind feels out of control. Children feel this more acutely than adults. Before our sons and daughters surrender to this realm, they need to be reassured of the solid truths that form the bedrock of their confidence in themselves and in their world. Their parents form part of this foundation. As noted in the chapter on toys, a teddy or a special blanket gives children the handles to hold fast to as they slide into the nocturnal landscape performing the same function for children as when they venture out into the world. The family bedtime ritual helps a child feel safe, protected, and loved as they separate from their parents.

The good bedtime story helps with this transition, for it promises the return of the dependable world as soon as the child awakes. And the nighttime story is told in close physical contact with mom or dad. The psychologist Erik Erikson suggested that the first task of each person is to sort out whom they can and cannot trust. The bedtime story ritual helps the child take on the lonely night equipped with the tactile memory of his or her parents' love and the imaginative inspirations of the story. The nighttime journey itself becomes part of the narrative. The dreamscape is no longer a strange land out of the child's control. When a child imaginatively gains control of her environment, she has been empowered. The bedtime story prepares her for novel situations that she can face with confidence, knowing that she is supported at home yet equipped to face any challenge outside the home.

Family rituals tend to come at transition times, which are the most tenuous part of a child's day. Dinnertime transitions the family from their public work lives back to the privacy of the home. Breakfast performs the opposite function. Bedtime, as we just discussed, prepares children to swing from the comfort of the evening to the inner recesses of their dreaming mind. You will find that your children are the most at risk in their lives when they undergo major transitions, say from high school to college or from being single to being married or from being a toddler to going to school. Ritualistic observances at these times (weddings, commencements, the first day of school) help pave the way by acknowledging the importance of these transitional events and gathering a sympathetic community for the sojourning child. Daily rituals, however mundane and frustrating they may seem, perform the same function for the small transitions of everyday life.

Modern families who are torn among so many competing obligations find it difficult to establish family rituals. When moms and dads work until seven or eight each night, it is next to impossible to have a family dinner. Many families I know—even many religiously devout ones—have given up going to church, because they are sleep deprived and just have no energy for another event at the end of the week. My own family rarely eats a meal together, though we do try to gather on Sunday nights.

Rituals do not have to be patterned on the traditional, typically mythical family structure we might see on old television shows.

The important thing is to establish a few key rituals that endow your day or your week with meaning. Ron Carlson's short story "The H Street Sledding Record" in his collection *A Kind of Flying* is one of the wisest and most sophisticated testaments to the importance of rituals in a family's life. It tenderly describes the nontraditional Christmas Eve rituals of a family struggling to find meaning and its place in the world. On Christmas Eve, since his daughter was four, the narrator in the story shovels a bushel of horse manure on the roof of his house to prove, in the morning light, that Santa's reindeer did indeed land there. His wife and his mother indulge him, though his wife worries that the "proof" will be so powerful that their daughter will never outgrow her belief in Santa and will, in high school, be ostracized by her peers.

> I have thrown horse manure on our roof for four years now, and I plan to do it every Christmas Eve until my arm gives out. It satisfies me as a homeowner to do so, for the wonderful amber stain that is developing between the swamp cooler and the chimney and is visible all spring-summer-fall as you drive down the hill by our house, and for the way the two rosebushes by the gutterspout have raged into new and profound growth during the milder months. And as a father, it satisfies me as a ritual that keeps my family together.

Notice that this passage includes images of family rituals, earthy waste, and dramatic growth. At its most basic and simple level, this is a story about a wife and husband deciding about whether or not to have a second child. They clearly have a happy marriage but seem ambivalent about how to balance professional ambitions with the needs and comforts of home life. The story is deliberately vague. We know the wife has attended law school and left a "firm" to stay at home with her daughter. The husband seems dreamy and, though well educated and sensitive, he does not appear to have ever entertained a career.

The husband loves rituals and spends the story recounting them. The word "ritual" appears in the story more than any other noun. This repetition becomes, if you pay attention, a mantra and a rhythm. We hear in lyrical detail how, each year, his family buys a Christmas tree, lays out the presents, makes a phone call to the mother-in-law, uses code words to initiate and refer to matrimonial intimacy, threads popcorn, decorates the tree, tells stories about their marriage before the advent of their child, and tries to set a record each year for how far their sled can slide down a main street.

"The H Street Sledding Record" is a great story for parents because, though it lovingly describes the unique and bonding rituals of a happy family, you get the sense that these rituals may be employed to hide from a reality they would rather not confront. It leaves you a little uneasy about the motivations of the narrator-father. The fact that the father sees rituals everywhere and in everything may indicate that he recognizes the sacred nature of his calling as a parent. It may also point to an existential panic; he may instinctively feel that emptiness resides at the core of the swirl of family activity. He courts and embraces all of his family-constructed rituals, and yet they seem a little too artificial and conditional. In fact, "condition" is the code word he and his wife use for intercourse. Their touching but elaborate Christmas routines may be blocking true intimacy. The story prods us to think more deeply about the place of family rituals. They are potent, for they both give meaning to our lives and potentially shield us from reality. Like formal religious rituals, family rituals are tricky because they can so easily slide into empty, formulaic expressions of sentiments that were once charged and in need of representation.

The work of spiritual people, whatever their religious tradition, is to notice. Instead of being caught up in the mind's fantasies and abstractions, a loving, compassionate soul sees the world in all of its detail—and in all of its detail, from horse manure to sunsets, the seeker awakens to the presence of God. Parents who seek the spiritual path notice all of the particulars of the child, including the pleasant and the unpleasant.

The most potent and living rituals force us into this kind of focused attention. Those rituals that have become hollow allow us to drift away from attending to what is at hand. Carlson's story teeters on the edge of this fault line in the lifecycle of family rituals. At one point, he describes how some of the shoveled manure missed the roof and smeared a kitchen window for the rest of the winter. Is the dripping manure a pun? Is Carlson saying that Christmas is really just a lot of horse manure? Or can this striking image of a ritual gone astray remind the family, even months after the Christmas season, of a father's dedication to preserving his family's structure, myths, and cherished truths? A streak of melting manure on a kitchen window does force us to pay attention; perhaps it is the mark of a still-meaningful ritual.

11

Gossip

WE BEGAN THIS BOOK BY ASKING ABOUT THE POSSIBILITY of knowledge. Parents are continually questing for certainty and for advice. They turn to professionals, such as pediatricians and teachers; to pundits, such as the writers of books and advice columns in parenting magazines; and to other parents. Whenever you see two or more parents together, cart to cart in the supermarket or face to face in the school parking lot, you can be assured they are trading insights and stories about their children.

Other parents serve vital functions for us. They can be clearinghouses of information. One woman I know, whose son plays hockey with my son, sits in the stands and dispenses advice on all things. She has opinions on the best dentists, the best schools, the best car washes, the best gourmet food stores, the best way to drive downtown, the best way to control your child's computer use, the best stores for sporting equipment. During a typical hockey game or practice, she will hold court and answer all parenting questions from the trivial to the existential. She always finds a willing and ready audience because we parents are essentially information traders. We think that the right tidbit will unveil the great mystery and make us more effective and efficient.

Sometimes parents do give good and useful advice. The other

day I confided to a friend that I thought my son was developing into a tattletale at school. I asked her how I should counsel him out of this bad habit. Having older children, she assured me that this was a natural behavior for a six-year-old. He would grow out of it, but in the meantime, she said, I should tell him that if he insisted on reporting on the activity of his peers, he should report the good with the bad. In other words, don't just tell on Johnny when he leaves the cafeteria without permission—also tell the teacher when Johnny scores a goal in the playground soccer game or writes a good story in his journal.

This was helpful not only because it was a useful technique, but also because she acknowledged that her children had gone through the same stage. When we find a shared humanity with other parents, our work as caregivers doesn't seem so lonely, nor do we feel so incompetent. Other parents can reduce our normal anxiety by reassuring us that we are not the only ones with a surly adolescent who hates our guts. All parents need to develop a supportive community of fellow parents to share the best practices and to heal our isolation. These are essentially the same reasons why Buddhists meditate with other Buddhists, Christians gather together to worship, and Muslims are called the world over at the same times each day to pray. Parents need each other in the face of the frightening void; we need to renew our calling; we need to share stories to inspire and to instruct; we need to explore what works and what doesn't work.

Sharing information is one of the most ubiquitous aspects of parenting; it is almost the life breath of being a mother or father. We share stories about our children so often that we rarely step back and notice how much storytelling is a fact of parenthood. Yet when parents gather to gossip or engage in what the German philosopher Martin Heidegger called idle talk, they face the dangers of misinformation and risk losing their spiritual calling as parents. In our quest to uncover the secrets of raising our children, we can develop bad habits. Gossip, at best unhelpful and at worst unethical, is one these unfortunate habits.

Anthropologists have suggested that gossiping is one of the distinguishing traits that make us human. Unlike other animals, we are by nature storytellers. Parents, in particular, compulsively weave narratives. (I am clearly one of those parents.) New parents love to chronicle the discoveries of their babies and toddlers. Using anecdotes, photographs, journals, videos, DVDs, tape recordings, and saved scribblings and scrawls, they create exquisitely detailed documentaries of the first time their son or daughter said or did anything. Sometimes these stories seem to be pointless. The other

~

New parents rediscover an almost primitive wonder of the world; as their children age, parents' stories about their children begin to take on a different, more noxious tone.

~

day a new parent excitedly told me that his two-year-old boy took off his own diaper and said "wet." I was tempted to ask "And your point is?" before I caught myself, realizing that I too was a compulsive parental historian (CPH). I know I bored my peers to death with amazing tales of my toddler's development, from his first belly crawl ("he actually squirms out of his pillow the minute we put him on the floor") to his instinctive feel for twentieth-century art ("he paints like Kandinsky").

It is not hard to understand why parents become CPHs. Some may say it's pure ego, but I think that, at least with the parents of young children, it's part of the spiritual awe we all feel when we first have children. Their movements, their habits, their unique being that appears out of nowhere does seem miraculous, and we want to catch and preserve the miracle on film and in print. We

are trying to capture the ineffable. The CPH has the religious
instinct of a prophet. He has witnessed a revelation, and he feels
that he must spread the good news with all of humanity. Religion
is sometimes defined as the communication of revelation. Parents
who relate their baby and toddler anecdotes are not braggadocios;
rather, they sincerely believe that they have witnessed something
unique, a kind of revelation. We listen patiently to their otherwise
mundane stories because we understand that they have accessed a
truth that is both purely personal and universal. New parents rediscover an almost primitive wonder of the world; they marvel that
there is something rather than nothing. They revel in the mar-
velous randomness of creation, and their gospels of crawling and
burping and pointing reintroduce us to a mode of innocent appreciation we lose almost as soon as we gain it.

Yet as their children age, parents' stories about their children
begin to take on a different, more noxious tone. It is one thing to
tell a story about your one-year-old naturally grabbing a hockey
stick and swinging it at a tennis ball. As the audience, we might
comment that she is clearly a natural athlete. It is entirely another
thing for a parent to tell you that their seven-year-old scored the
winning goal in his hockey game and that he's headed for the
NHL. As the audience, we feel that this parent is pushy and
immodest. Why is the baby story charming and the seven-year-old
story boorish? I think it's because the first story is a mode of
beholding, and the latter a mode of aggrandizing. When we talk
about our babies and our toddlers, we seem to be focusing on the
miracle of creation. As children age, stories about them become
more stories about ourselves. And so they take on aspects of bragging. By the time our children are thirteen, our stories take on the
characteristics of a résumé. Hence, CPHs move from universal
tales of awe and wonder to chronicles of achievement that attest to
the superior genetic makeup of the parents, to recitations that
sound like mere rehearsals for their upcoming college applications.

As our child changes and grows up, our ego becomes more a character in the stories we tell about her. Gossip is one aspect of this progression of parental ego. As your child ages, you are more likely to gossip because your social network of associations increases, as does your child's. The older they get, the more your son and daughter will bring a store of gossip-worthy subjects to your attention. Day-care centers, nursery schools, elementary schools, high schools, colleges, teachers, school administrators, other children, other parents, coaches, sports teams, extracurricular activities, pediatricians, hospital emergency rooms, vacation spots, summer camps, siblings, extended family members, babysitters, television shows, movies, games, Web sites, toy stores, clothing outlets—all of these are gossip-worthy, and the list grows with each year of development.

As stated above, parents need each other to provide comfort and advice about all of these topics. Parental conversation turns into gossip when we talk about other people in a negative way and without their permission. Usually, gossip involves relating the misfortunes of another person; it can also take the form of revealing the negative characteristics or evil intentions of that person. It is true that we sometimes gossip about an institution or a large group, like a school or a sports team or a country or a family, but chatter about an aggregate is really about the people who comprise it. When I complain that the New York Yankees are too old to win in October after playing such a long season (and they are, by the way), I am maligning their players, not the abstract team. Gossip always concerns other human beings. We don't normally say that when people are talking negatively about animals they are gossiping. I may complain about Fred's barking dog, but my complaint is actually about Fred and his inability to control his pet.

Gossip is almost always immoral. But since it is almost a biological drive for most people, we tend to disregard the moral dimension of idle talk. Unlike most other forms of unethical behavior, the victim is not present when he or she gets assaulted. This lack of physical proximity makes gossip seem harmless.

What's more, gossips are usually clever wordsmiths, and they can veil malicious gossip using a variety of literary sleights of hand. While advising me about a building situation at my school, a fellow headmaster told me a story about the worst gossip at his school (a parent we'll call Mr. Green), who always couched his most vicious attacks as charming personal narratives or stories of battles for truth and justice. For instance, over the weekend, part of the roof in the school's kindergarten collapsed, releasing a small amount of asbestos. Seeing the gravity of the situation, the headmaster immediately hired a certified asbestos-abating company, decontaminated the room, set up a phone tree to alert the parents, and sent out an official letter explaining the situation. Before he received the letter, Mr. Green received a call from a school volunteer who said that part of the roof had fallen, but there was no asbestos. The caller meant that there was no asbestos in the room because it had already been cleaned.

Mr. Green told a different tale as he took it upon himself to call the other parents. He explained that he was a contractor, and he knew that buildings of the same age as the kindergarten contained asbestos. Since part of the roof had fallen, Mr. Green reasoned that asbestos must have been released. Since the volunteer said there was no asbestos, his fertile mind concluded that the school must be engaged in an asbestos cover-up. He told this story numerous times over the course of a day, trying to rally a group to investigate the situation. His narrative was intended to reveal (a) how smart he was, (b) what a knowledgeable contractor he was, (c) how much in the know he was about events, and (d) how corrupt the school must be.

Thankfully, the moral of Mr. Green's story was disrupted when the other parents received the school's letter, which frankly detailed the situation. The headmaster told me, with relief, that the other parents had begun to question Mr. Green's motivation, for they had learned from experience to trust the school's credibility.

Mr. Green disregarded the truth and acted out of hostile intent. Consider the possible truth conditions of one who gossips. The gossip either knows all of the facts of the story he is relating, some of the facts, or none of them. Regard the motivations of the gossip. He intends either to demonstrate his superior knowledge (an egotistical intention), to malign the reputation of a person or an institution (malice), or to enlist aid to help solve the problems of the person discussed in the gossip's story (genuine concern).

If you graph these possibilities, there's only one instance in nine where it is ethical to gossip or to exchange information about a third party with another person, and that is when you know all of the facts and sincerely desire to help.

THE ETHICS OF GOSSIP

Intent	Level of Facts		
	Truth	*Some Truth*	*No Truth*
Ego	X	X	X
Malice	X	X	X
Concern	***	X	X

The next time you feel the need to gossip, consult this chart. Be honest about your intention. Reflect on whether or not you know enough of the facts of the story you are about to relate. If accuracy and ethics are important to you, you should only proceed if you are motivated by a deep concern and desire to make a situation better and to help another person or institution, *and* if you are sure that you know the whole truth and have access to most or all of the facts.

In *Being and Time,* his mammoth analysis of the various modes of being in the world, the German philosopher Martin Heidegger describes idle talk as one of the ways humans drift from a true, authentic engagement with the world. Gossip, or as Heidegger puts it, "passing the word along," negates the possibility of genuine understanding. It is a mode of communication driven by others rather than by an honest and direct connection to the object of our concern.

This is the very antithesis of spirituality, which in any religious tradition is characterized by a longing for an intimate connection to the very ground of our existence. A spiritual parent seeks a type of knowledge that is not refereed by other people or a society's rigid prescriptions. Gossip as a way of knowing is just another manifestation of our drive to control and to predict, rather than to celebrate and to understand. Rabbi Joseph Telushkin tells the Talmudic story of the snake defending itself. Humans accuse the snake of poisoning other animals not for food or survival but for sheer pleasure. In his defense, the snake points out that humans do the same thing with their gossip, which only humiliates and destroys others. Hence, the spiritual parent who truly longs for a deep connection with their children and with all of creation must always guard against gossip. And since it's an insidious and normal dimension of everyday communication, one must be ever vigilant.

The narrative form has been analyzed in many ways by scholars, as a mode of knowing that is circular rather than linear, metaphorical rather than literal, and universal rather than particular. Stories click with our brain much better than a list of facts or analytic arguments do. These are some of the reasons why great teachers like Jesus chose parables rather than writing academic treatises or conducting sociological surveys.

But we give too much credit to the narrative as an authentic way of communicating, as though every story was worth listening to. When my wife and I first moved to Buffalo, we attended a neighborhood picnic. Mrs. Sands approached us, and began to tell us the story of her niece's orientation at a local college. Mrs. Sands went into rich detail about how much she enjoyed the orientation and, knowing that we were both academics, she wanted to extol the virtues of the college to us in case we had never heard of it. And just in case we hadn't been convinced by her enthusiasm and her storytelling skill, she concluded with the following thought: "It was so wonderful being with those young adults. For once the college didn't force the diversity thing. They were all white and so well dressed; they looked just like a J. Crew commercial!"

People are by nature storytellers; stories and narratives are an important way of coming to know our culture, our universe, and ourselves. Yet, Mrs. Sands's racism is not healed by the fact that she expresses it as a story. Stories only give a certain form to information; bad or malignant information, and information maliciously interpreted, is always bad or malignant, no matter how engaging or entertaining its story is.

If the gossip chart has any validity, then 8/9ths of the gossip or idle talk you hear is a mixture of ignorance, malice, and egotism. Along with books and television shows and conversations with pediatricians, parent-to-parent chatter is one of the primary ways parents seek to understand their children and themselves. If, then, this parent-to-parent communication is mostly idle talk, then parents who seek spirituality are swimming in toxic waters whenever they speak with other parents.

Parents need, then, to converse rather than to gossip. The Latin root of conversation means to transform and turn around. Ralph Waldo Emerson often makes a connection between an authentic conversation and a conversion. He does not mean conversion in the sense of one person imposing upon or breaking the will of another, but rather in the sense of transforming both of the souls of the conversationalists. In his essay "Friendship," Emerson writes: "Great conversation requires an absolute running of two souls into one." True conversation is spiritual because, as Emerson says in "The Oversoul," "in all conversation between two persons, tacit reference is made, as to a third party, to a common nature. That third party or common nature is not social; it is impersonal; is God."

When two or more parents sincerely speak with the goal of discovering a truth beyond social conventions and a truth beyond the yearning for power—a truth that is, in other words, transcendent and thus transformational—they have successfully avoided merely "passing the word along." The spiritual parent seeks these Emersonian conversations as an essential part of their path. She is indeed blessed to find another parent who is conversant rather than a mere conversationalist. Happily, we don't need to remain silent until we find our ideal conversation partners. In the meantime, we know what kinds of talk to avoid as we seek a more enlightened path.

12

$\mathcal{I}$nterests

When Henry was just about seven, he joined a Little League baseball team. He had never played organized ball, though we had played a lot in our backyard. Henry had always been a shy boy, and I was a little wary because none of his friends from school were in the league; the boys on his team would all be strangers from different schools and neighborhoods.

At his first practice, Henry marched boldly onto the field and took his place in line for a hitting drill. On the first pitch, he smacked the ball all the way out to the outfield, to the astonishment and glee of the coach. In the field, Henry caught every grounder and pop fly that was hit to him. He also mastered a throwing drill, in which each player had to try to pitch the ball to a small target. The coach said, "Henry, you're going to be our rookie of the year." Near the end of the practice, the other boys surrounded him and slapped him on the back. One said, "Henry, we're so glad you're on our team. You're our best player."

Perhaps you smell the noxious fumes of CPH braggadocio, but indeed I was so proud of him. No boy or girl on either side of our family had ever done particularly well in sports. Henry was the first Frome at any age to receive peer recognition for athletic accomplishments. What was more important, I was delighted that he could participate with a bunch of new kids without blinking an eye. It seemed to me that he had matured and grown in confidence.

But then Henry nearly broke my heart. When I asked him how he felt about the practice, he responded, "Do you think that you get an award at the end of the season? Do you really think I'll be rookie of the year?" Henry considered the coach's turn of phrase, which was only meant to encourage a newcomer, to be a promise of glitter and gold at the end of the season. Rather than a love of participation and camaraderie, my son appeared to have more superficial motivations.

Henry came to associate playing sports he loves with individual awards because of an earlier experience, one that had had a much deeper effect on him than I realized. In Buffalo, as in many northern climates, children take up ice hockey at a young age. Henry began to skate at the age of five. (Inspired by the example of his older brother, our youngest, Spencer, started at age three.) When Henry was four, he begged for rollerblades, so we gave him a pair for his birthday. Since no one in the family could teach him how to use them, he just put them on and began to shuffle up and down the driveway. Where this drive to skate came from, I have no idea. Hockey is the dominant sport in Buffalo; it's on local television all the time; children in kindergarten knowingly argue about why our NHL team, the Sabres, continue to lose and may never be able to win. The NHL lockout has broken our spirit. I'm sure Henry was responding to the culture of his hometown. Yet, this does not entirely explain why he pushed himself so hard to learn how to rollerblade. He fell and skidded and slammed into the garage door each day. Soon enough, though, we detected a glide here and a glide there. He began to push out with one leg, gaining strength and speed. Before the summer ended, he had become an adept little skater.

That winter he studied every televised hockey game he could find. He didn't care if it was the local high school team or an obscure college game. Henry loved the game, as did many of his peers, and he began to understand things like icing and offsides.

For his next birthday, he asked if he could join an ice hockey team. We signed him up for a summer skills clinic, invested in expensive equipment, drove him out to the rink, tied up his skates, and watched from the stands as, for the first time, Henry put blade to ice. Remarkably, he took off around the rink without falling. As he completed his first lap, he made his way to the bench and sat down and wept. These were not tears of joy, but of horror and fear. The coaches gently tried to coax him back on the ice, but he was too overwhelmed by the size of the rink, the expertise of the other boys and girls, and the sheer reality of what had been a mere idea to him all winter.

I walked down to the bench to see if I could comfort him. Henry looked at me and sobbed, blubbering that he just wanted to go home. I was torn among conflicting thoughts, some noble and others more base. On the noble side, I wanted to teach Henry the value of trying hard, conquering fear, carrying through on a commitment. I also, though, was thinking about the hundreds of dollars we had just invested in hockey equipment and camp fees. Hockey parents are not the gentlest community, and they were already snickering at how the headmaster's son was crying. I was embarrassed and furious, and I wanted Henry to stand up for the honor of our family. I knew that poor Henry's fear was already being broadcast by some of the leading gossips in our community. These thoughts may have been normal for a dad to have, but they did no good for Henry.

I told Henry that it was okay if he didn't play, but that he would have to sit on the bench for the rest of the practice to support his teammates. He pleaded with me to take him home, but I stood firm. Why did I make him stay? In all honesty, I took a stand on principle (the value of commitment) in the hope that he would get bored on the bench and go out and skate, showing the others how talented he really was. This admixture of values and ego is not uncommon for a parent, but I'm not particularly proud of it. I do believe that one's motivations color one's achievements, and the end of Henry's young hockey odyssey will bear this out.

Henry did indeed tire of sitting, and he eventually shuffled out onto the ice. From that moment on, he loved to play hockey and, indeed, he developed a passion for playing and for studying all sports, from baseball to soccer to basketball to pool. Henry did well for the rest of the camp. At the end, the coaches gave out several awards. Henry won a T-shirt for perseverance. As he proudly walked up to receive his award, one of the veteran parents snickered in my ear that our son had won an award only because the coaches were trying to recruit us to join their winter league.

The coaches kindled a confidence and a hunger in our son, and he did join the team for their winter season. We all got up at 6 AM every Sunday morning to get him to the rink and dressed for the 7 AM ice time. Henry practiced hard, and my wife and I began to fall in love with a sport that could inspire such responsibility and diligence in a five-year-old boy. When the season ended, the coaches hosted a formal awards dinner at a fancy restaurant downtown. After dinner, each little boy and girl was called up to get a certificate for participation. As they walked up to the podium, they passed a table loaded with silver medals and statues, eyeing it with desire as they returned to their seats.

After the certificates were distributed, the head coach announced that the big moment had arrived where the major award winners were to be announced. The children were riveted. So were the parents. The first award was to be given to the rookie of the year. The coach read the list of nominees. To our astonishment (and excitement), the coach read Henry's name. After a dramatic pause, the coach announced the name of another boy as the winner.

As we drove home, I asked Henry if he knew what it meant to be nominated. Without pause, he replied, "Yeah, it means you lost." Like most young children, he could cut through our adult pretensions and view the situation with simplicity and clarity. It's true that even Academy Award nominees are essentially the losers. I regained my balance and explained that to be nominated for an award was a great honor. Writers and filmmakers and athletes who don't win but are nominated are considered to be tops in their field. By extension, I told Henry, he should be proud of his nomination and understand that his coaches saw him as one of the best players. He perked up. Being only five and still struggling a bit with articulation, he announced to his mother and brother, "Did you hear? I was dominated!" For the rest of the summer, when asked how he enjoyed hockey, he bragged that he had been so good, the league had dominated him.

The way youngsters struggle with the language often reveals deeper truths. Henry's introductions to awards at such a young age did indeed "dominate" him. The next year, he attended almost every practice, skated on an outdoor pond for hours in sub-zero weather, played against older children, and studied professional games whenever we would allow him to stay up late or I could get Sabres tickets. When we attended the awards ceremony the next year, we warned Henry that he was no longer eligible for the rookie of the year award. We also explained that having so much experience but still being so young made it highly unlikely he would even be "dominated" for anything this year. Still, he sat on the edge of his chair throughout the night. He patiently paid attention to every award, even the ones for the kids in the more advanced leagues. He made us stay through to the bitter end. His name was never called. As we walked out to the car, I asked him what he thought of this year's ceremonies. He said, "I guess I had a bad year." Again, we tried to put the whole awards issue into perspective for him, but he was not developmentally ready to understand any of my words. For him, you either brought home a statue or you stunk.

I didn't realize how much this earlier lesson had soaked into his bones until the next spring, when Henry's baseball coach called

him rookie of the year at the first practice. I tried to explain to
Henry that sometimes people used the phrase just as an expression
for someone who does well with only a little experience. I lectured
that the only reason you should play a sport or learn an instrument
is for the sheer enjoyment of it. I told him that people who do
things only for awards usually don't win the awards. Henry kept on
saying, "Yes, Dad, I know, Dad." Knowing that he was blowing me
off, I got more frustrated, and finally delivered an ultimatum.

"If you are playing baseball only so that you are going to win
an award, then I'm taking you off the team."

Henry parroted, "No, no, no . . . I really like to play. I promise
I won't talk about awards again."

I knew that my words had only nicked him skin deep. Henry
knew me well enough to say what I needed to hear, even though
he believed I was fundamentally confused about the nature of
competition and how people measure their own worth.

I still think I am right, though. Successful people are people
who love an activity in and for itself. Successful artists, athletes,
teachers, mechanics, bankers, doctors, and lawyers are committed
to their particular field as a fascinating end in itself. They are successful because they are perpetually hungry. Their skills and
achievements follow from their appetite. Since successful people
are literally starving to do their chosen activity, work is their
reward. The story goes that Willie Mays was shocked when he
received his first paycheck for playing baseball. He couldn't
believe that someone would pay him to play a game that he loved
and had played for free his whole life. Rewards and awards, if they
come, are merely byproducts of the passion of a successful person.

Every parent should facilitate and guide their child's search for
their passion, whether it is watercolors or carburetors. This is really
a search for the core of their selves and for the meaning of their
lives. Unfortunately, our culture is not structured for such a search
toward personal authenticity and quiet happiness. Our children

live in what I call the "getting-in" culture. Like an odorless gas, the assumptions of this culture pervade the lives of most educated middle- to upper-middle-class families today. It is marked by an obsession with marketing our children so they can gain entrance to elite colleges and universities. The main idea is that the more competitive the institution is, the more likely you are to have career success. (Bonus: The more elite the school, the more bragging rights the parents enjoy.)

~

Because participants in the "getting-in" culture think that marketing and packaging are the beginning and end of life, they are almost always disappointed.

~

The "getting-in" culture embraces marketing as a way of life and as an end unto itself. In this culture, we use our selves, our experiences, and our aspirations as products to be packaged and positioned. Volunteer work in a soup kitchen, for instance, is performed not in and for itself as an altruistic deed, but as a commodity to be sold later to a college admissions officer. The commodity becomes the very self of the applicant. I am afraid that an entire generation of parents have become stereotypical "stage mothers," primping and protecting their children as they do everything and anything to build their little résumés.

To see the self as a product to be molded and shaped for an exterior end is clearly antithetical to any religious sensibility. If the common element of the world's major religions is selflessness and humility, then our "getting-in" culture is decidedly unspiritual. Any parent who seeks to parent from a spiritual base must be on guard against this culture—indeed, ready to march head on and do battle with it. If I come to see my self as a mere product, I lose the chance to be an authentic human being. I stand in danger of losing my freedom, which, as I have suggested throughout this book, is the greatest spiritual gift our children have. It allows them to escape the clutches of mechanistic logic and recipe-following parents and institutions.

Most contemporary Americans don't realize that marketing does not work without authenticity. Any good advertising executive will tell you that marketing techniques without a substantive product to sell may gain short-term attention but will ultimately fail. (Think of all the Internet companies that vanished almost overnight.) Eventually, customers will determine the true nature of a product, and then they will use that most potent marketing instrument, word of mouth (i.e., gossip) to dethrone it. Before they create an advertising campaign, the best marketing firms work with their customers to determine what is unique and special about the products they are trying to sell. They will then determine if customers perceive that unique quality; they will then devise ways to get the message out more effectively.

Because participants in the "getting-in" culture think that marketing and packaging are the beginning and end of life, they are almost always disappointed and resentful. Even if, after thirteen years of résumé building, you gain access to Harvard or Yale, you still may wake up in the morning feeling empty. At the end of her first year at Harvard, one of my advisees asked me how she could experience the "real" Harvard. I was stopped by the metaphysical implications of her question, so I asked her to clarify what she meant. She told me that she had wanted to attend Harvard her whole life. Visions of Widener and the Charles River had danced in her mind ever since she could remember. Now that she was at the school, she had participated in many classes and activities in order to bring Harvard as close to her as possible. But she was always left unsatisfied and unfulfilled. She didn't feel like she was anywhere special at all. It was all so ordinary. That year, in fact, the ivy had been stripped off the walls of the buildings in Harvard Yard because it was eroding the brick. Even the dominant metaphor and moniker for schools like Harvard—the striving, climbing, encircling, evergreen, and darkly romantic ivy—turned out to be just a weed, and an insidious nuisance at that.

My advisee was trying to embrace a chimera, an unfaithful lover. How could I explain to her that Harvard was just a collection of brick buildings and blackboards inhabited by smart, intense people who were subject to the same petty jealousies and insecurities as everyone else? Grades, hockey, painting, dance, martial arts, Habitat for Humanity, the lead role in the school play, summers in the south of France, and backpacking trips in South America were regarded by many students as potential planks in a college application platform. Spontaneous activities, like playing touch football in the neighborhood or quietly strumming a guitar in the basement, were considered too lightweight even to mention. Thus, my advisee had never enjoyed a deep engagement with life or herself. Too many of our children and young adults are stumbling around like aging existential philosophers who acutely suffer from the meaninglessness of their endeavors.

To avoid this too familiar feeling of ennui and emptiness, parents must dedicate themselves to raising children who have authentic and passionate interests—which will make them, by definition, interesting children. The philosopher John Dewey distinguished three types of interest:

1. Interest as an occupation or activity, as in the sentence, "Miles has business interests in London and Singapore."
2. Interest as that which can have a negative or positive influence on your well-being, as in the sentence, "Miles has a silent interest in Sarah's corporation." This definition would also cover the sense of interest as a financial gain on an investment or loan.
3. Interest as that which absorbs us or wraps us up in a pursuit wherein we lose ourselves unselfconsciously, as in the sentence "Lorraine was interested in all vertebrates since she could walk."

Dewey notes that the root of the word "interest" means to be in a state of being in-between. Being in-between is just another way to talk about growing. When I am in the process of growing, I am between one state and another, more mature state. It is a wonderful, thrilling feeling to be in-between; we should be in-between our entire lives, for then we would always be in a state of becoming. People on a spiritual quest are in-between, always going but never getting there. This is the wisdom of the Buddhist monk, Lin Chi, who told his followers that if you meet Buddha on the road, you should kill him. And this is why Jews and Muslims and Christians are reminded to not worship idols. Anything final destroys spirituality.

Too often, our ways of parenting and schooling are predicated on the second sense of interest. When teachers state that they want to make a lesson interesting, they really mean that they are seeking to entertain or to give the students an immediate reward. Such "interesting" teachers are rarely celebrated because they have inspired their charges to dwell in the spiritual excitement of being in-between, on a journey of self-discovery. Parents, too, treat potentially inspiring interests, such as dance or music or painting, as literal investments, which they hope will bear a good interest rate in terms of scholarships, college acceptance letters, and monetary rewards.

If we dedicate our lives to nurturing the third sense of interest in our children, they will inevitably succeed. Literally, they'll get to the next step of the sequence of growth. The students who actually do get into elite universities, for the most part, pursue their studies and their activities because they love them in and for themselves. They are truly interested in the genetic morphology of the CR1 immune protein and would be studying it whether they were in a famous lab at Harvard or forced to stay home and attend the local community college. Helping children cultivate this mode of interest, which transcends ambition and competition and even natural aptitude, is the key to their happiness, to their success, and to breaking the grip of the "getting-in" culture.

I have heard so many parents brag that their child is in the "gifted and talented" program at their local school. Instead of designating certain students as "gifted and talented," I would push schools to create "passionate and interested" programs with the goal that every child would become a P & I kid. My first wish and hope as a parent is that my sons will become interested in something—anything, whether carburetors or Plato or right angles or woodwind instruments or the traffic patterns on Main Street in Buffalo (which are in terrible need of synchronization). I wish that all of our sons and daughters will experience the bliss and blessing of being swept away by a pursuit so that all that matters is the activity itself, in all of its beauty and logic and sense of possibility. This feeling is in essence identical to the love of God and of creation and of being alive. In such a state of authentic interest, you are unburdened of the demands of the ego; you can give yourself up to the joy of being "in-between"—aloft with your own sense of potential and wonder. In this state, it is not the race that counts, but the ride.

I am pleased to report that Henry's Little League baseball season was long and fun. There was no more talk of awards. He was given opportunities to play each position. He fell in love with being a catcher. By the way he pounced on balls hit in front of the plate and the way he casually tilted the catcher's mask up to watch a play develop in the infield, you could tell that catching somehow hooked into an authentic part of himself. He got to play a few games in the older league, where he faced great players and fast pitching and learned to go down swinging with dignity and a resolve to hit the damned ball the next time. At the end of the season, there was no awards banquet. Instead, we hosted a pool party. The boys ate pizza and swam, and their parents played a particularly spirited whiffle ball game in the backyard. Everyone seemed to be betwixt and between.

13

Questions

"What would happen if the sun exploded?"

"Why does a toilet need water?"

"If there was no time before time, how did people tell time?"

"What happens after you die? Where do you go?"

"Is there a medicine you can give a dead person to bring them back to life?"

"Who made the earth?"

"Why do we have commercials?"

"Who was the first dog?"

"How are television shows made?"

"Where do colors come from?"

"What is the last number?"

"Is China next to Canada?"

"How come you can see the moon when the sun is still up?"

"What makes wind?"

"If God is everywhere, is he in this tree? This bug? This stick? This piece of dirt?"

"How are houses made?"

"Who is more powerful, Daddy or God?"

I CHERISH THOSE MOMENTS WHEN ONE OF MY SONS IS SCREAMING for me from some part of the house and I run to his aid, thinking that the plumbing has backed up or an appendage has been severed. I find him sitting quietly. I ask him what's wrong and he says, his voice sort of corkscrewed up and sing-songy, "Dad, I've got a question." For the duration of rumination, these questions tend to shut down the business of the house, whether it is cleaning or throwing the baseball or driving to the grocery store.

You never know when these questions will arise or what will stimulate them. When Henry was three, he participated in his preschool's Christmas pageant, which included a reenactment of Jesus's birth. After the show ended, as we were walking back to the car, Henry told me he had a question. I geared up for some sort of theological query, but instead, it turns out the Immaculate Conception had struck Henry on a biological level.

"Where do babies come from?" he asked.

It occurred to me, for the first time, that the Christmas story invites this most basic and most profound of human questions as much as it points our attention to matters of the infinite and the spiritual.

Some schools have a designated time in their schedule called Stop-Drop-and-Read. In our household, we Stop-Drop-and-Ponder, whenever we can. No matter how busy I am and no matter how entangled the question, I always force myself to stop, to listen, and to respond. Though it's hard sometimes, I try my best not to be dismissive.

Why? The growing tumult of children's questions as they gather developmental and linguistic momentum is, I believe, one of the most sacred aspects of childhood. Childhood questions are not just mental gymnastics. Neither are these wondrous inquiries and insights necessarily the signs of a budding astrophysicist or priest. Children's questions represent their first inklings that there is a greater universe out there. There is something beyond the circle of the ego. These questions are, at heart, the beginning of humility, the most basic and important religious value. In these questions, children implicitly acknowledge forces greater than themselves. They acknowledge that they occupy a tiny spot in the cosmos. They acknowledge that they are ignorant of many things. And, at the same time, they begin a heroic quest for understanding in spite of, and in light of, their own human limitations.

Once, a question swooped out of nowhere and socked me in the gut and changed my cast of mind forever. I was in the third grade. I was walking down a set of stairs when it occurred to me that space was infinite. I had pondered the dimensions of space before and settled on the solution that a wall or some sort of barrier rose up at the end of space. On this day, though, apropos of nothing, I realized that this final wall too had dimensions. It had thickness; it had to exist itself in space. Something had to be behind it. Space could not be stopped! This thought rendered me dizzy and nauseous. I literally felt as if I had been punched in the stomach by the insight of infinity. I remember falling back, catching myself, and sitting down with a hard thud. I felt different and a little ashamed, like I had just peeked into a forbidden closet that contained adult secrets.

I have since come to know that my experience was not unique. Most children confront the idea of infinity at some time in their elementary school years. In the Everyday Math Program, first graders spend the entire year making number scrolls, where they write in sequence as many numbers as they can on reams of paper that they tape together to form a rolling scroll. Many kids get into the thousands by the end of the year. With this concrete exercise, the children happily take on the Sisyphean task of counting continually and get a taste of the vastness of infinity.

Parents tend to squelch the natural torrent of questions from our children, for a number of reasons. First, the questions can be truly annoying, especially when the questions topple out of their mouths one on top of the other. "Why is the sky blue and not yellow?" "Why do we have to eat?" "Where does the poop go after you flush it down the toilet?" "How do airplanes fly?" We are trying to get something important done, like putting up an unwieldy patio umbrella, and the children distract us with their unrelenting inquiries.

Second, these questions make us confront our own ignorance and limitations. In many cases, we just don't know the answer. No matter how many times I look it up, I can't explain how an airplane flies. It's just inconceivable that something so big and heavy can get off the ground. Of course, we don't like looking vulnerable and confused in front of our children.

Even when we know the answer, we often get tongue-tied trying to put the explanation into lucid terms that a four-year-old can understand. The other day I smartly fielded a question about the contents of water. I decisively answered, "Two parts hydrogen, one part oxygen." I should have seen that this answer would automatically lead to a flurry of questions about hydrogen and oxygen and how you slice them into different parts and what they look like when they are just by themselves and who does the slicing into parts. I could not simply and elegantly define the periodic table of elements for my four- and seven-year-old boys that would in any way satisfy them. Some questions are uncomfortable as well because of their subject matter. How can I explain why my son's friend's father died, when I don't have any clue myself?

Third, many parents think that these questions are just a waste of time, representing idle chatter. This takes us back to the dominant epistemology of parenting, namely mechanistic thinking. If the goal of parenting is to concoct a recipe for successful and happy children, with both success and happiness being determined by various modes of external validation, then random metaphysical thoughts and idle philosophical questions don't seem to be necessary or helpful. They are too much vanilla extract for the batter. We fear that if we give our children's questions our attention, our kids will turn into dreamers. They will wander off task. They will accomplish nothing. No one gets rewarded in school, in society, or

at work for asking why things are the way they are, we think. In
any case, what if they discover that the universe is absurd? What if
they uncover the emptiness of existence? This will only depress
them and further inhibit their achievements.

Children's natural questions are anathema to our culture
because we don't regard parenting as an opportunity for reverence
and deep understanding. In Jonathan Lethem's wonderful novel
The Fortress of Solitude, the painter/struggling single father, Abraham Ebdus, describes his approach to art: "I prefer not to speculate. That's the daily task, in my view. A refusal to speculate, only
encounter. Only understand." Most parents, including myself,
spend more time speculating—that is, trying to figure out all of
the angles based on "if-then" logic. If I indulge these questions,
will my daughter become depressed and overwhelmed? What if I
give the wrong answer?

When Henry asked me, after the Christmas pageant, where
babies come from, I gave him a scientific answer. When I told his
teachers about the conversation, they scolded me, explaining that
he was not developmentally ready for my reproductive biology
lesson. I should have told him a story, like "the stork delivers
babies." I felt terrible and, using my "if-then" logic, I worried that
I had screwed up sex for Henry for the rest of his life.

The philosopher Gareth B. Matthews has written a trilogy of
books (*Philosophy and the Young Child; Dialogues with Children;*
and *The Philosophy of Childhood*) that analytically and experientially make the case that children are natural philosophers not only
because they instinctively pose questions that academic philosophers recognize as the proper subjects of philosophy, but because
children restlessly seek answers. Society and its educational institutions fail to nurture the child's inner philosopher, and thus most
children lose this instinct over time. Matthews makes the case that
we can study a philosophy of childhood in order to examine our
preconceptions and abstract assumptions about what we mean

when we talk about children. These are important books for all parents and educators to read and to embrace.

As an analytic philosopher, it falls outside Matthews's discipline to meditate on the spiritual dimension of the child's native instinct to ponder. As a philosopher with analytic training myself, I admire how close his books do get to this subject. If we throw off the restraints of analytical philosophical techniques, we can be more blunt. Children's questions are not just philosophical urges common to most of humanity—they are instances of hierophany. They are the first pecks of an ego trying to break out of its self-referential shell.

The automatic questions of children are the first expressions of wonder. In the Platonic dialogue *Theaetetus,* Socrates says: "for wonder is the feeling of the philosopher, and philosophy begins in wonder." This is in response to young Theaetetus's complaint that his head "quite swims with contemplation." Even the rationalist Plato sees the connection of this feeling of wonder to a spiritual sense of awe. Socrates makes the point that Iris, the messenger of heaven, is the child of Thaumas, or wonder. Philip Fisher once noted that in the English language, wonder means two things that bridge philosophy and a religious sensibility. "Wonder" as a verb means to be perplexed and to be propelled to discover an answer to a question: "I wonder why the sun looks orange today?" As a noun, wonder refers to the experience of awe; something is so miraculous and new that it defies explanation: "Marcia's skating is a wonder."

Raising children involves, of course, both senses of the word. They are a wonder and they make you wonder. In this word "wonder," we discover the oscillation between the religion of parenting (beholding, acknowledging, and thanking the miraculous) and the science or the philosophy of parenting (reducing the mystery to a set of understandable and controllable variables). As Fisher explains, to have wonder is to come upon something that we can take in as a whole in one gulp. We experience this as parents when we behold our newborn. In these first minutes of life, we spend most of our time looking and watching. But then, she starts to cry. She cries all night. She doesn't ever seem to sleep. You start to wonder why. You call your own parents. You buy parent advice books. You visit the pediatrician. Notice that the more you wonder, the more you drift away from your initial wonder.

~

Raising children involves both senses of the word. They are a wonder and they make you wonder.

~

I believe that when children wonder at an early age, they brilliantly inhabit both senses of wonder. The two senses can be analytically distinguished, but in the experience of the child they are undivided. When my four-year-old asks where the sun goes at night, he is curious and at the same time in awe. This is true for all of the young children I see at my school. When children are young, curiosity and celebration are intertwined. As they age, as schools and society focus on developing their intellects, as we emphasize achievement over process and discovery, the twin senses of wonder unravel and separate. The great geniuses of the world, from Socrates to Einstein, manage to keep the senses of wonder together. They investigate and marvel at the same time. This is the theoretical aim of the Waldorf education curriculum as well. These schools, started by the German scientist of the spirit, Rudolf Steiner, attempt to teach their students to engage in science, art, and reverence as essentially the same activities. For most of us, though, the minute we begin to wonder, the backdrop of wonder starts to fade.

I think children, along with many great artists and scientists, are able to hold on to both kinds of wonder because they see the world as new at all moments. The writer and comedian Tony Hendra's spiritual advisor, Father Joe, taught that the new is the eternal as opposed to the recently acquired. He says, as quoted in Hendra's spiritual autobiography, *Father Joe*, "The world worships a certain kind of newness. People are always talking about a new car, or a new drink or p-p-play or house, but these things are not truly new, are they? They begin to get old the minute you acquire them. New is not in things. New is within us. The truly new is something that is new forever: you. Every morning of your life and every evening, every moment is new. You have never lived this moment before and you will never again. In this sense the new is the eternal." It takes adults of all spiritual disciplines years of practice to recover this sense of newness. It comes naturally and with each breath for a child.

Why is this? First of all, children are growing so fast and in so many different directions—cognitively, physically, emotionally, and experientially—that each day is dramatically different. At forty, you will probably look the same next year at forty-one. Not so at six. At seven, your teeth are falling out. Your pants grow shorter every day. Your face changes shape. You start to become more aware of the implications of things. On a daily basis you may swing from one set of friends to another and from one set of interests to another. Last year, you were a hockey player headed for the NHL. This year, you can't stand the bitter chill of an ice rink, but you love the turf of a soccer field. You were once a dancer, but now you're a painter. In a few years, your entire body will transform. You will develop reproductive capacities. Your emotions will unwind.

Imagine if, at forty, you experienced the same rapid rate of noticeable change as you did in elementary and middle school. As you turn forty-one, you need a whole new wardrobe. You're taller now. Suddenly, you lose your teeth and a new set comes in. At forty-two, you tire of being a banker. You tell your spouse that from now on you're going to be an astronaut. At forty-three, your friends have all changed too, as has your spouse, and you find that you have nothing in common with anyone anymore. You gravitate to a new set of acquaintances. At forty-four, you begin to think differently. All of the ways you understood and categorized the world now seem silly and childish. You adopt a new worldview. Your vocabulary grows. You can hurt people with words now, and you try out some of your new powers (and then lose the job at the bank before you can quit).

I dare say that such rapid change as an adult would scare you and thrill you at the same time. You certainly would be questioning what's going on, and at the same time, you wouldn't be distanced from your question. Analytic thought, philosophy, and science are all marked by distance and impartiality. As a forty-something changeling, you would be your own question. You would be wondering at the wonder of you and the wonder of it all. It would not be pleasant to be this way, but at the same time you would be fully engaged with your world.

Pregnant women are perhaps the only adults who have this experience of rapid physical and emotional change and its concomitant anxiety and excitement. But this is the everyday experience of children. This is how children commune with the eternal, for everything is new. Change never stops. As the Greek philosopher Heraclitus is reported to have said, you not only cannot step into the same river twice, you can't even step into it once.

The paradox of childhood wonder is that while all this growth and transformation are occurring, one of the most persistent questions children have is about death. The children I know and teach often inquire about the afterlife and the beforelife. The other day, Spencer asked where he was before he was in his mother's belly. Why is it, in the tumult of daily development and newness, that children are so interested in birth and dying?

It is almost cliché to note how much of children's literature focuses on death, dying, and loss. From Bambi to Harry Potter to the Lion King, the characters in children's movies and stories are constantly losing their parents. There is a genre of television shows I label "Mom's dead, let the adventure begin!" *Full House* is an exploration of the nutty antics that ensue when three guys try to parent three girls after they lose their mother. The Brady kids only come together to make a fun-filled family after the boys and girls each lose a parent. The popular animated movie *Finding Nemo* begins with the death of the clownfish mom—and then dad and son have the adventure of a lifetime! *The Courtship of Eddie's Father* is another classic television show about the comic implications of a widower father. We can argue whether all of this death in children's entertainment reflects the anxieties of children or causes them. It is undeniable, though, that death is a dominant and persistent theme in children's entertainment.

Even though most children do not live on farms anymore, where death is as much a part of daily life as cultivation and fertilization, death does permeate the everyday experience of suburban and urban children. In my school administration jobs, I've had to deal with death and dying more than I ever expected. Children face the death of pets all the time. They lose grandparents. Some lose their parents. Students lose their friends. In every school I've ever worked in, from the college to the kindergarten levels, teachers and administrators have been forced by circumstances to confront the reality and the meaning of death with their students.

As a graduate student, I never would have expected or predicted this, but now that I look back on my career, part of my informal job description as an educational leader is to attend funerals and to try to make sense of them for my faculty and students. Having never attended a funeral as a child, I now spend a significant portion of my time as headmaster going to them. As I write this, I have attended three funerals in the last month on behalf of my school. Two were for grandparents and one was for the parent of two of our young students. Other students and their parents and their teachers attended these funerals. It would be absurd to think that we could shield our children from the existential questions of finitude when they are as much a fact of their lives as eating and sleeping.

But even if a child got through her early years without reading the bulk of children's literature, or losing a pet, friend, relative, or parent, or without knowing someone who did, she would still be aware of and interested in death, for the simple reason that she would know she had been born. Every family has a story. The story involves mom and dad meeting, courting, and then having a child. This story is told over and over again and it hangs in the air of all families. It is the umbrella-narrative for your child's life and provides the framework and groundwork for the development of his or her identity. The logic of a beginning, though, is that it entails an ending. So, if children are acutely aware of where they come from, and interested in where they were before even that, they're going to also be concerned about where they are heading.

So amid the swirl of growth, children recognize death. In an earlier chapter, I noted that William Blake defined the creative imagination as a place where "Contrarieties are equally True." Wonder is just another word for this kind of imagination, where the child is able to hold in her mind at the same time the seeming contradictions of life and death. The psychologist Carol Gilligan characterizes adolescence as a time of mourning for the lost childhood self. Adolescents, she teaches her students, are like Miranda in *The Tempest*, for they suddenly find themselves shipwrecked on a strange island. Growth entails loss. The fourteen-year-old young woman is no longer a girl. The kindergartener is no longer a toddler. The toddler is no longer a baby. Parents celebrate the progress and feel the loss as they cry when they drop off their son for his first day of school. Children inhabit this cycle of perpetual shedding and growth, of commemoration and lamentation, of thrill and melancholy. It is the source of their wonder and their hunger to wonder. If children have any wisdom to teach adults, it is that, even though we may seem settled and finalized, we too tread this cycle.

14

Schooling

You can tell a lot about parenting styles by observing the way parents drop their kids off at school or at the bus stop. Every day I stand at the front door of my school and watch the students arrive with their parents. There are so many ways that families say goodbye to their children for the day. Some pause in the car for a few minutes before the child opens the door and steps out. Others slowly stroll in together. Many times the children run down the sidewalk with their parent huffing and puffing behind. The temporary parting of these families serves as a window into how the family is dealing with the inevitable reality of separation and maturation. Some mourn it; some fear it; some celebrate it; some accept it; most parents are just ambivalent as their once-toddling toddler firmly marches into the kindergarten. Parenting is as much about saying goodbye as it is about nurturing and caring and preparation. School is where parents say their first goodbyes.

When I ask parents what they want most for their children, they inevitably respond that they want their sons and daughters to be happy. They mention happiness before academic skills or preparation for life. Happiness seems to be the primary parental goal, yet it is a poorly understood concept. For thousands of years, philosophers have debated what it means to lead a happy life. Psychologists and brain researchers have applied empirical methods to studying what makes happy people happy. But there is little agreement on the definition of a happy person, and without agreement on the meaning of the concept, it is difficult to agree on what to study.

I'm going to resist writing about schooling and happiness, for that would take an entire book. But let's talk about schooling and spirituality, leaving for another time the question of whether a spiritual life and a happy life somehow inform each other. Throughout this book, I've suggested that we parents are blocked from fully appreciating the spiritual dimensions and lessons of raising children because, in our attempt to understand childhood and to do the best for our children, we employ reductive, "if-then" recipe logic. Though this kind of thinking has its place, it inhibits the fullest use of our imaginations and thus restricts our ability to see, to hold, and to behold our youngsters in all of their freedom and particularity. There is no space in the dominant parenting paradigms for the eternal.

Schools, both public and private, teach, institutionalize, and ratify this mode of rationality at the expense of other more imaginative and spiritual modes of thought. Schools are where the twin senses of wonder are separated and segregated. In the best schools, pupils are encouraged to wonder about things that can be measured and analyzed. Finding and beholding a wonder is never part of the curriculum; I have never seen a mainstream school that evaluates its students on their ability to wonder and to imagine. In any case, the evaluation of wondering is probably an oxymoron. Still, reflect on your own schooling and the schools your child attends. I would bet that mystical ways of knowing are not nurtured or encouraged.

Some philosophers of education will argue that the role of school is to support society. Since our society runs on a service-technological economy, we need to produce workers who think in quantifiable, logical ways. We need an analytic citizenry that will increase productivity. If this other way of thinking is so important, they suggest, then let artists and families and priests and rabbis teach it. Schools should not be in the business of creating mystics.

Other educators believe that schools should be in the business of transforming society. Schools should teach their students to think well and freely and creatively. In so doing, children will be liberated from the domination of society's institutions. Since human freedom is the highest value for democracies, schools can only support our society by engendering free thinkers. Creating servant-like automatons, so this line of argument goes, only promulgates oppression and makes our culture stagnant and, in the end, undemocratic because it limits human freedom. Teaching children to make meaning, according to these thinkers, ought to be the primary goal of education.

Though I have simplified the debate, every thoughtful educator oscillates between these two poles. On the one hand, we want every child to experience success in the society she will enter. Since a radical spiritual and epistemological cultural revolution seems a rather distant possibility, we feel the need to equip our students with the best skills to thrive in the kind of society we do have. If we can't liberate their souls, we reason, at least we can give them choices. On the other hand, teachers, at least at some point in their careers, do want to change the world by nurturing thoughtful, questioning, and creative children. And good teachers see each child for the individual he or she is. They resist stuffing students into cookie-cutter categories. Most teachers I know detest standardized tests, especially the ones prescribed in the No Child Left Behind Act, because it forces them to ignore the particularities of each student. Since their school is evaluated only on the criterion of the test score, teachers feel that they must drum uniqueness out of their curriculum. Jill, the lovely fourth-grade poet and good friend to all, becomes simply Jill, the below-average reader who along with her below average cohort drags the school's reputation down and agitates the principal.

Supporters of No Child Left Behind and testing in general will counter by saying that we do no service to Jill if she cannot read or calculate. Even if your aim is to liberate her soul, mathematical and linguistic literacy can only make her freer. And so the debate continues.

Looking at the way schools operate is perhaps the best way to address the questions of this book. Schools are where the needs of society and its predominant ways of knowing, and the emotions and confusions and celebrations of parenting, meet head on. While we want our child to conform to exterior standards of growth and maturity, parents also recognize, more than any authority, their unique and glorious status. If parenting is not a recipe, we at least want some guidelines. At the same time, if children can just be boiled down to a set of instructions and outcomes, why does this feel so wrong and misguided? Schools rarely see their task as mediating this tension between the mysterious and miraculous nature of the child and her need to work within the contours of cultural expectations. To return to an earlier metaphor, if kindergarten is a garden, what kind of garden is it? Is it a grove of carefully sculpted bonsai trees or a wild and abundant eighteenth-century English garden accented here and there with touches of planned color?

In the early grades, most schools do address the unique qualities of each child. As the students age, schools begin to concentrate on their roles as the producer of efficient, skilled workers. Some schools may bridge the two poles by saying that a post-industrial economy needs and will reward free, creative thinkers, and they gear their curricula accordingly. This is really a thinly veiled solution. These schools are still in the business of serving the needs of America's workforce. There's nothing wrong with schools that serve the workforce, of course; they should just be aware of and honest about what they're doing.

Schools need to serve both goals, for teachers are working with miracles. Of course, these miracles need to read and do math. Part of every student's sacred nature is that she loves to learn until she is taught to hate to learn. When schools ignore the divine nature of their charges, or say that it is not their business to address the spiritual side of their students, they are choosing to ignore an enormous part of the very material they're working with. It would be like an auto mechanic who never looked at the engine or the axles, but only tried to fix a car by adding gasoline and changing the oil. Or like a painter who knew how to mix colors but had no feel for canvas.

I know, I know—these analogies are reductive and encourage, once again, seeing children as products. Schools, by their very nature, discount and discard the spiritual. If we really take the reality of hierophany seriously, and we genuinely see our children as hierophanies, then how can educators separate the sacred from the material when they are teaching children, without missing something essential? If the really real *really* is hierophantic, then schools that focus only on the contingent and the measurable are creating fictions—disconnected, virtual universes that can only inspire disconnected, virtual selves. Disconnected, virtual selves hardly ever do much good in the world; their karma, as it were, is mostly negative. In the previous chapter, we characterized wonder in part as the appearance of the unexpected. Schools are wary of the unexpected and are constructed to prevent it from happening. The curriculum is a tool schools use to ensure the expected. We will study X and then study Y during these years and at these times, and then we will undergo these tests to prove that we studied X and Y during these years and at these times. Hence, by definition, schools exclude wonder, the joyful beholding of the appearance of the unexpected, from their environments. In so doing, they wean their students from their spiritual nourishment.

Mystics from all religious traditions teach that there is a difference between the self and the soul. The self, or the ego, divides and distinguishes itself from the rest of the world. The soul recognizes no such distinctions. It communes with all of creation—past, present and future. The soul finds its ground and its nourishment in this identification. Once we begin to make distinctions between me and you, us and them, matter and spirit, past and future, my country and your country, life and death, we begin to lose our souls, for we lose the sense of connection and union.

∿

When schools ignore the divine nature of their charges, they are choosing to ignore an enormous part of the very material they're working with.

∿

If this is true, then it should come as no surprise that the academic curriculum would fail to feed the souls of its students. Academic rigor is defined by the practice of making and discovering analytic distinctions. The day is divided into periods; the curriculum is divided into different, discrete subjects; the school is organized according to distinct departments. Students vie for awards and recognition and admission into prestigious universities. A close friend of mine heads the admissions office of a very competitive college. He says that his job is to increase the stature of the college by rejecting as many applicants as possible while still filling the beds of the dormitories. Given this standard of success, he says that his actual title should be "Dean of Denial" rather than "Dean of Admissions."

This anecdote serves as a metaphor for the thrust of our education system. It is about weeding out, rather than weaving together. I just attended the commencement exercises of a girls' high school. The bulk of the program was dedicated to recognizing the students who won an award or received a financial aid package from a college. The winners were all asked to stand. The rest of the class (about half of the girls) simply sat, staring straight forward. This tableau of standing and seated young women, each draped in a white gown, clutching a bouquet of roses, represents our educational system and practice. Us and them. Winners and losers.

Mel Brooks once said (in a sardonic tone) that it was not enough for him to succeed; someone else had to fail for him to feel good about his success. Schools tend to take the sarcasm out of this comment and then measure their students accordingly. How and for what purpose does the school evaluate its students? The answer to this simple question will not only tell a parent what matters to a particular school, but will illustrate how a school deliberately and unconsciously organizes and creates its culture. If a school measures success by elite college admissions, then its entire system, both social and academic, will be constructed to meet this goal. If a child's success is predicated on how well she does on state standardized tests, then those tests will determine the scope and sequence of the curriculum. If you take a melon baller to a melon, you wind up with only two things: melon balls and the hollowed-out husk of the melon rind. The same holds true for students and their schooling experiences.

So how do you educate to nourish the connectivity of the soul and still build academic skills and help children become productive, thoughtful members of society? I can only pose the question and point to a potential response by telling the story of a remarkable nonprofit organization called College Summit. Each summer, College Summit helps thousands of inner-city high school students complete their college applications and, each winter, it helps them navigate the admissions process. Seventy-five percent of their students matriculate, more than doubling the normal rate for this population. While this may seem like a perpetuation of the kind of competitive, soulless education we find in more affluent schools, the College Summit curriculum achieves its goals within an environment of mutual support using a curriculum that encourages each student to develop their unique voice by telling stories. College Summit does not distinguish between but combines the quest for personal authenticity and the desire for worldly success.

Surprisingly, despite a K–12 school system standardized by testing and large textbook companies, college admission officers still search for students who differentiate themselves by personal passion and sincere interest, in the sense of interest defined in chapter 12. College Summit recognized this contradiction and exploited it. Knowing that the personal stories of inner-city students would capture the imagination of the typical college admissions dean, the founder, J. B. Schramm, created a program that would promote the personal essay as the centerpiece of his students' applications.

The College Summit workshop takes place on a college campus. The participants are inner-city high school students who wish to go to college, but are C and B students with low SAT scores. Mentors and teachers escort them from their high schools or youth groups or churches. Over four days, the students, who are grouped into teams of five or six, meet with motivational coaches, college counselors, high school advisors, and writers in order to develop a list of appropriate universities to apply to, and to complete a college application with a polished, striking personal essay that exhibits, in the terms of the program, "heartbeat." These essays, and the support of the loving and nourishing community that the summit engenders, distinguish the program and catapult the students ahead.

I have had the privilege of teaching at several summits, and I think that they present a paradigm for a healing educational program. The students are members of a team, not a class, and the curriculum demands the support and encouragement of each teammate in order for everyone to succeed. In other words, individual achievement is a community goal. Students work their way through a writing process that encourages introspection. It's a process that acknowledges that writers do not know what they want to write about until after they have written. The curriculum also recognizes that writers rarely compose alone, but create within a community of supportive editors and fellow writers. After each stage of the writing process, the students share their work with their group partners. Their colleagues are taught to interpret and react to these drafts; their reactions orient the direction of each student's next draft, which is then shared and revised.

And so it goes. Under the guidance of a writing coach and other teachers, these essays are gently sculpted to take analytic shape, but never at the expense of authenticity and personal passion. At the end of three days, each student produces a polished personal statement. I don't think there has ever been a College Summit workshop where a student has not produced a worthy essay. On the night of the third day, all of the writing teams come together for a banquet where excerpts from each essay are read aloud. I have never in any other educational institution witnessed the sense of pride and achievement and emotion (and the absence of hurt feelings and divisions) as I have at these banquets. Though the College Summit placement rate is impressive, the professionals who volunteer at a summit are more impressed with the unique atmosphere that the workshop engenders. It is a form of communion.

These students' essays pound like beating hearts. They echo, for they are grounded. Listen to some of this work:

My brother Sali and I are in the living room watching Barney and *Sesame Street*. There is loud banging on the door. I hesitate to open it; my mother always told me not to open the door for anyone. But the knock becomes louder and a woman calls out: "Open the door." Terrified, I obey. As I slowly open the door I see a blond haired, skinny woman. She is dressed in a navy blue uniform. On the far left side of her chest she wears a sophisticated gold and silver pin. On the far right side of her chest she has a nametag that says, Officer Terry. Her eyes are ice blue and her hair braided in under her police hat. "Are you alone?" she demands.

—Dorina Arapi

And . . .

In the languages of my ancestors my name is xwi-pam, which means Evergreen Flower; in my Catholic religion I was baptized into this world as Magdalene Nicole Kelly-wood. I am from high atop the Sangre de Cristo Mountains, where the air is moist and the sun is heart-warming, in a pueblo, which is a small village, called Picuris.

—Magdalene Kellywood

And also . . .

He was given to me about seven years ago for my birthday. Yellow, white, green and black were the colors that covered his soft-feathered body, His songs were so delicate and beautiful that sometimes one would think that they were in Egypt or some other exotic country.

—Kpodon J. Patterson

College Summit encourages these students to sound like themselves. For many, this is the first time an institution has said to them: "It is not only okay to be yourself. In so doing, you will succeed." This is said with words and by the ceremonies and structures of the summit workshop. It is proclaimed loudly and whispered quietly, and you can tell that the students hear it by the subjects they choose to write about and in the cadences of their sentences. They have been liberated.

College Summit succeeds in its mission because its curricular rigor serves a spiritual vision. It goes back to the problem of epistemology discussed in chapter 1. Most schools adopt the same instrumental epistemology that guides parenting advice books. They see children as recipes and regard success or failure as measurable. Hence, most schools ignore vital characteristics of human beings and fail to recognize the spiritual aspects of childhood. College Summit combines instrumental reasoning with a more spiritual mode of knowing. The program's goals are precise and measurable, just the way administrators and politicians like them to be, but they are achieved within an inclusive, loving culture that respects and values the integrity and unique spirit of each student. Without any adherence to an overt religious tradition, the summit workshop creates the elements of worship: community, rituals of celebration, a belief that all are worthy, communal work, a spirit of hope, and the expectation of the unexpected to arrive and change lives. The writing curriculum itself prizes the unexpected and celebrates true wonder. Each essay is a wonder produced by students who have been allowed to wonder. In so doing, paradoxically, each student fulfills our society's prescription for success, namely, college admission.

Your child's school is your parenting partner. If you have the choice, seek a school that attempts to go beyond a reductive epistemology not only in what it teaches, but how it teaches and how it organizes its community. Parents who yearn for a more holistic and celebratory mode of raising their children struggle to paint a spiritual backdrop that stands in relief to all of their child's normal activities. It is an understanding that, like the figures in a bas-relief, distinguishes our everyday actions. We need to give schools permission to adopt these deeper ways of knowing and understanding the world, and thereby contribute to the spiritual relief of our lives with our children.

15

*I*njuries, Falls, Sickness, and Failure

IN JOHN GARDNER'S NOVEL *NICKEL MOUNTAIN* (WHICH is unaccountably out of print), a new father, Henry, expresses his anxieties to an old man, George. George says: "You take on a responsibility like that, and you say to yourself you'll move heaven and earth to protect the kid you love, or the woman, or whoever it happens to be, but the minute you say it you're forgetting something."

Henry asks, "What's that?"
George pauses and responds: "You can't."
Henry laughs a little and says, "It's what drives you to God."

This exchange sums up the very idea of this book. Parenting is not about control. It's the heroic attempt to protect, nurture, and define your child, along with the recognition that however much you try, you can't. It's about what not to expect.

And within this tension in trying to do what we know we can't, spiritual wisdom can be found. Every parent will experience daily moments of being out of control. You go out of your way to create a wonderful summer experience for your four-year-old. You enroll him in an expensive day camp in a lovely school. You cajole the mothers of his friends to send them to the same camp. Including his closest friends, the camp has everything he loves: swimming, sports, cookouts, arts, and animals. Everything is perfect and in its place as you leave him off the first day.

He comes home that afternoon and announces that he hates camp. You call the director. She says that he had a great day. Indeed, he led his entire group through the halls singing "Jingle Bells."

You point this out to your four-year-old. You remind him that he gets to spend the whole day with his best buddies. He stares you down and begins to weep, rebutting, "But, but . . . I hate camp!" The next morning he refuses to get out of bed.

Most parenting books deal with this situation by suggesting certain gimmicks and tricks for getting the boy to go to camp without making a scene. "Try tough love, or sending him with a favorite toy, or try simple bribery." I think it's more important to notice that in this everyday, normal tussle the spirit is asserting itself. We are reminded that we are not, really, in control. Our child is free and sensitive and separate in the world. Controlling tricks may get him to camp in this instance, but these techniques, when used alone, will only serve to miss the deeper dimensions of your role as a parent. I'm not arguing not to try to get him to go to camp, but your relationship with your child will become more meaningful when the techniques you use to get him to camp are played out against a backdrop of spiritual understanding.

Most parents experience the feeling of being out of control when their child is suddenly injured or seriously ill. These moments tend, with a loud thud, to bring down the backdrop of the great, terrifying reality that life is fragile and our existence so tenuous. Almost every parent at one time or another experiences this frightening confrontation with our ultimate existential state. It can begin suddenly, late at night, with a cough or a cry or the ringing of a phone, and play itself out in an emergency room.

My family is not unusual in this regard. During the birth of our second son, Spencer, his heart began to beat irregularly. My wife, Ermelinda, had been in labor for thirteen hours when Spencer's progression became jeopardized. Our obstetrician, who sat through much of the ordeal knitting in a rocking chair like Madame LaFarge, told me we'd have to think about doing a C-section. My wife and I started to discuss the pros and cons of this procedure, when I noticed that the doctor looked more serious than ever. She rushed around, mumbling to the nurses, and left the room. As a physician, my wife quickly understood there was something wrong with Spencer. As a patient, she started to panic. Our doctor quickly returned, reporting that she had called for assistance. My wife needed an emergency C-section because Spencer was quickly losing blood pressure. She asked if I wanted to be in the room. I did. I scrubbed in as they prepared Ermelinda for the procedure.

I noticed the new ob-gyn as I was escorted into the operating room. He was an older man in scrubs who was also eyeing me. We continued to look at each other for a few seconds, then he broke into a wide smile. He walked over to me and slapped me on the back. In my own numbed state of panic, it took me a few seconds more to notice that he was our neighbor. The day before, we had stood together at the foot of my driveway discussing the Buffalo economy. I immediately relaxed, went over to Ermelinda's side, and told her that it was going to be okay because Dr. M was here to do the C-section. She smiled—I think she smiled, that is—and then told me that she didn't really care who did it. Within minutes, Spencer was delivered—breathing, bloody, and seemingly content.

My wife and I were overcome with relief. At that minute, we became fervent and faithful worshippers, sincerely thanking God for Spencer's deliverance. A few hours later, our pediatrician visited the new baby. As she held him in her arms, she told me that he was so beautiful she needed to be alone with him undistracted and asked if she could take him with her. I knew by her offbeat request that something wasn't right. I played along and let her go, counted to five and then surreptitiously followed her through the hallways. She collected a few nurses as she walked with Spencer in her arms; they took him into a room with large glass windows. I kept my distance and watched as they gathered around Spencer and turned out the lights. In the dark room, I saw a small speck of light dart sideways and up and down and then suddenly disappear. The lights went back on, the door opened, and I rushed back to my wife's hospital room.

~

Parents are really not in control; the unexpected is the only expected. Our children are separate from us.

~

When our pediatrician returned, I confessed to her that I'd followed her. Being my neighbor and friend, she told me that she wasn't surprised. She said that Spencer was okay, but that she thought she had seen an abnormality in his eye that could have indicated blindness, so she felt that she needed to perform a more extensive examination without alarming Ermelinda and without my hovering about—hence the ruse about the need to be alone with the beautiful baby. We thanked God again.

Our newfound piety began to wane as we brought Spencer home. His first weeks were tough, and my wife had a particularly difficult and painful time recuperating from the C-section. She could not go up or down the stairs, and she was constantly aching. In addition, Spencer was a difficult breast feeder. As headmaster, I couldn't entirely ignore my work, so I struggled to keep the school running and to tend to my family as well.

Schools tend not to forgive administrators and teachers their private lives. I delegated as many duties as I could to my division heads, but I still felt guilty and torn that I couldn't focus just on the needs of my wife and sons. After three weeks, Spencer began to take to a routine and Ermelinda began to feel better. We were sitting on our patio on a warm, bright early spring evening. Ermelinda was holding Spencer, and I was watching Henry run around the backyard. The best weather in the United States occurs in western New York in the spring and summer. It's both lush and cool. Our yard was a mixture of dark and light greens with pockets of gold and yellow flowers. I remember sitting back and thinking that the good life was about to come rushing in. Even though there were still trivial administrative issues that distracted me, my school had settled down too. I felt an almost physical sensation of things falling into place, and I began to relax. Ermelinda and I looked at each other and smiled.

If you ever get that feeling, start to dread it. Truly, just as peace and harmony had descended on us, Ermelinda stopped smiling and said, "He feels warm. I don't have a good feeling about this." I dismissed her worry as paranoia, but I should have known better. As the night progressed, so too did Spencer's fever. We had to take him to the emergency room. The fear was that he had a bacterial infection.

Most likely every parent spends some time in an emergency room, where our primal fears meet antiseptic bureaucracies, unhappy and underpaid interns, and residents locked in power struggles with unhappy and underpaid nurses. This clash of parental anxiety, institutional inertia, and professional sullenness is played out in a barren, whitewashed interior design suggesting prisons or old public schools.

It is here that parents, especially new ones, dramatically face the underlying reality of their job—we are really not in control; the unexpected is the only expected. Our children are separate from us and, despite our most Herculean efforts, they will suffer. They may even die.

To rule out a bacterial infection, Spencer had to spend a night undergoing painful tests. They took blood and urine samples, but the lumbar puncture was the worst. We were not allowed in the room, but his screams and cries pierced the solid door as we waited outside. The experience of a parent witnessing extreme pain in his or her child is an awful and helpless mixture of distance and absolute connection. You feel the pain as if it were your own, with the full awareness that it is not your own. It is a double shot of physical trauma and existential impotence and despair. I don't relate this anecdote to solicit sympathy, or out of a sense of heroism. In the annals of parenthood, this episode turned out to be a relatively mild adventure. We were so very lucky—Spencer just had a virus. And he has grown into a strong and vigorous little boy, though he still goes to the emergency room from time to time. Every parent can tell a story like mine. Every child will, at one time or another, get sick or injured. Most of the time, they will recover. Sometimes they do not survive. Sometimes they are stricken for a long period of time. All of these experiences present a spiritually significant lesson for parents, if only we open ourselves to see and to receive it. When our children are sick or injured, we are brought face to face with the awe-inspiring, overpowering, and potentially awful ultimate reality that delineates our essential imitations. Philosophers and theologians call this reality the "sublime."

I always associate that spring evening on the back patio with a short essay titled "The Sense of the Beautiful and the Sublime." It's crystal-clear writing from Immanuel Kant, an eighteenth-century philosopher who is usually a quite difficult read. Kant calls those sensations which we find pleasurable, the "beautiful." On the other hand, we feel "sublime" sensations when we are moved by a power that is greater than our own, reminding us of our own humble place in the vast cosmos. Kant argues that we cannot have a sense of eternity and the sacred without having

experienced the sublime. This experience is not necessarily pleasurable and can often be terrifying, as we suddenly realize the
fragility of our existence. Kant puts the distinction well:

> Great oak trees and lovely spots in a sacred grove are sub-
> lime. Beds of flowers, low hedges and trees trimmed into
> shape are beautiful. The night is sublime while the day is
> beautiful. Temperaments which have a sense of the sublime
> will be drawn toward elevated sentiments regarding friend-
> ship, contempt for the world and toward eternity, by the
> quiet silence of a summer evening when the twinkling light
> of the stars breaks through the shadows of the night and a
> lovely moon is visible. The glowing day inspires busy effort
> and a sense of joy. The sublime *moves*; the expression of a
> person experiencing the full sense of the sublime is serious,
> at times rigid and amazed.

Standing on a mountaintop is a sublime experience. If you fall,
you will die. The mountain's height overwhelms you, juxtaposing
your puniness against the magnitude of nature. Its peak seems to
come out of nowhere. The mountain will stand long after you are
gone.

It is not coincidental that these are also the emotions associated
with becoming a parent.

Kant goes on to distinguish three types of sublime experiences:
the terrible, the noble, and the magnificent. The terrible horrifies
us, because it forces us to confront death and the great void. The
noble sublime is always quiet and inspires us to admire the
majesty of the divine. The magnificent sublime illustrates the
ultimate beauty and order of the universe. In contrast, the beautiful is merely pretty. It is fleeting and small.

For many, the sublime reorients our attention to God. Psalm
90 speaks of God's awesome, frightening, and mysterious power.

His power is seen as a refuge. It can also be horrifying as when the hope of the resurrected grass in the morning dew becomes the despondent wilted grass of the afternoon sun.

> O Lord, you have been our refuge
> Through all generations.
> Before the mountains were begotten
> And the earth and the world were brought forth
> From everlasting to everlasting you are God.
> You turn man back to dust,
> Saying, "Return, O children of men."
> For a thousand years in your sight
> Are as yesterday, now that it is past,
> Or as a watch of the night.
> You make an end of them in their sleep;
> The next morning they are like the changing grass,
> Which at dawn springs up anew but by evening wilts and
>   fades.

When parents confront the sublime, they do not necessarily come away with a Judeo-Christian concept of God. But, as Kant argues, they will catch a glimpse of eternity, and it will give them pause. Can this pause become more than a moment? When the sublime grabs our attention, will we take away a religious insight that will inform the rest of our lives as parents and serve as our spiritual bas-relief?

It's easy for parents to notice the beautiful aspects of their children. Holiday cards exhibiting your son or daughter dressed as Santa's helper or driving a sleigh or rollicking in fall leaves are expressions for our parental search for the beautiful. When I was sitting on the patio, after Spencer came home for the first time, I only noticed beauty—the pretty flowers, the shaded grass, the contented infant snuggled against his mother's breast. I realize now how fleeting this sensation was. Instead, the terrifying sublime took the place of the beautiful. I was forced to confront my child's mortality and my own powerlessness. Every parent will have this experience at one time or another, and this is why, if for no other reason, parenting is essentially a spiritual journey.

Recently, two friends of mine told me stories that will always stay with me, because they so clearly represent parenting experiences as different aspects of the sublime. The first characterizes the terrifying sublime and includes aspects of the noble. Edward led a charmed life. The son of a notable family, he attended the finest independent day and boarding schools. Tall, athletic, and smart, he graduated from an Ivy League college and went straight to one of the best medical schools in the country. After his residency, he joined a prestigious private practice in Manhattan and moved into an apartment on Park Avenue. Edward soon met a pretty, articulate, and razor-sharp New York University graduate student who was just finishing her Ph.D. She eventually became a college professor.

They married and settled in for what they thought would be a traditional, happy life. Edward told me that they planned to move to a larger apartment in the city and purchase a country house for weekends and summers. Much as they had grown up, their children would attend the best schools, travel, enjoy long and loyal friendships, and choose interesting and satisfying careers.

These plans were put into perspective when their first child was diagnosed with cerebral palsy soon after she was born. In addition to the mental and physical stress of having a child with this disease, the parents were also subject to the added agony of never really being able to predict just how severe their child's condition would eventually become. Edward told me that it was this uncertainty that was hardest for him.

We had a long conversation one day about Edward's experiences as a father of a child with cerebral palsy. I will never forget it. He went into great detail about his family's navigation through the medical world, as well as his daughter's and his wife's day-to-day challenges. Edward said that the experience, though horrible and terrifying, had taught him that his previous values and priorities had been misguided. Schools and careers and addresses were ultimately empty. He prayed that his daughter would someday be able to walk. He would be thrilled and count his daughter's life a success if she could just do that.

Edward told me that many babies with cerebral palsy are unable to respond to their parent's coos and cuddles. His daughter, though, could smile back at him when he smiled at her. Edward counted the fact that his daughter could respond to him as the most tremendous blessing of his life. In the simple formula of smiling and smiling back, Edward revealed to me the entire meaning of parenthood. He taught me that the joy of parenting comes from the give-and-take between you and your baby, between you and your toddler, between you and your little girl, between you and your adolescent boy. It is the forging of a deeply connected, tenacious, never-ending relationship that is the miracle of parenting. Edward was profoundly thankful that he could give a smile to his daughter; that she could receive it; that she could let him know that she got it; that she could give a little of it back to him.

The other story of the sublime is much less dramatic, but I retell it in the spirit of hierophany. In the smallest of everyday happenings, if we are not awake and aware, we might miss a hint of the noble sublime.

Terry is a grandmother who shares in the caretaking of her three-year-old granddaughter, Molly. Molly calls her "Tutu." Tutu's family owned a house in Canada in an idyllic setting on Georgian Bay. Since she was a little girl, Tutu had spent part of her summers there, swimming, hiking, reading, and just being. Her son and daughter had spent their summers there, and now she was looking forward to passing on this almost spiritual inheritance to her granddaughter. Tutu shared the property with her sisters and their families, who increasingly saw the place as a financial and time burden. It was a long drive from Buffalo, and it needed a lot of upkeep.

Her siblings voted to sell the property despite Tutu's pleas. After the sale, Tutu, her husband, and Molly traveled to Georgian Bay one last time to close the house and move out. During that weekend, Tutu took a break and sat on the porch, looking out on the water. She told me that she had long resigned herself to the sale of the homestead. She was just admiring the beauty of the place and enjoying the scenery. It was a passing, fleeting moment. Molly walked out and joined her on the porch. She began to talk to Molly, pointing out different aspects of the bay. Molly turned to her and said, "Let's just be quiet, Tutu."

Terry told me that she hadn't discussed the depth of her feelings about her family's home with Molly. She had refrained from crying; she and her husband were treating the move as a grand adventure. Molly just knew, though, probably because of her intimate connection with her grandmother, that something important and sad was going on.

For Tutu, Molly's call for quiet instructed her to stop and to notice the sublime. What was passing through her grandmother's heart was inexpressible. It deserved silence, not words. Words would only sully her feelings. The wise child knew that this was a sacred time and spot. Quiet was the only appropriate sacrament.

Tutu realized then that she and her granddaughter enjoyed an unspoken connection that would last through eternity. In this small moment, she glimpsed the noble sublime. It was an insight that would always stay with her. And so Tutu held Molly closely, and they watched the sun play across the water.

16

*L*ove and Community

―――――――――――――――

A PLAQUE HANGING AT HARVARD DIVINITY SCHOOL
commemorates Ralph Waldo Emerson's famous and controversial
"Divinity School Address." The plaque, located in the Divinity
Hall Chapel where Emerson gave the sermon in 1838, quotes
from the text:

"Acquaint thyself at first hand with Deity."

When I was a student at Harvard, I heard this sentence used
time and again to prove that Emerson hated community (that is,
he was supposedly advising you to find God on your own) and
that he distrusted ministers (that is, no one else can show you
the way.)

The plaque, though, misquotes poor Waldo. He was speaking
to students who were about to become ministers. The actual sentence reads, "Yourself a newborn bard of the Holy Ghost—cast
behind you all conformity, and acquaint men at first hand with
Deity." While today, we would say the more inclusive "people"
instead of men, the actual sentence directs ministers to acquaint
their congregations to the immediacy of the Divine. Rather than
rejecting the need for community, Emerson calls for ministers to
join the fellow seekers in the congregation for a daily search for
revelation.

Just as (in the last chapter) Molly helped Tutu uncover a sublime moment of connection, regret, and joy, parents who seek the
spiritual need other sojourners to help them see. As Bob Dylan
once put it, we need others to help us look for our "lo and
behold." This is truly Emerson's message. The spiritually questing
parent turns the phrase "seeing is believing" on its head. Instead,
believing is seeing. In our culture, though, this is a strange and
foreign way of coming to know something. This is why we need
support. We need others to keep us on task in order to witness
what is truly revealed every day and in each moment.

Many books that discuss religion and parenting inevitably end
with a checklist or a "step-by-step" guide to becoming more spiritual, thereby repeating the instrumental reasoning that clouds
our ability to see and appreciate our daily revelations. I will not
end with a list, but with a call for a community of sympathetic
parents to get together wherever they may find each other and
acquaint each other at "first hand with deity." We tend to segre-
gate spirituality within the confines of the walls of an organized
religion; we are nervous to speak of the divine and the ineffable as
part of everyday life.

I recently was corresponding with an organization devoted to
helping teachers and parents gain more skills and understanding
of the needs of young children. The organization told me gently
but firmly that I couldn't present any part of this book at their
annual conference because they feared that I represented a faith-
based outlook and that they would lose their state funding if I
spoke. I responded that if raising young children did not include
an element of faith, I fear that all is lost.

By faith, I don't mean adherence to a specific theology or
notion of God. I do mean a hope for the future and an astonishment at the wonder of creation. Most secular schools and child
advocacy organizations ignore the status of the spirit in parents
and young children, and are hostile to and fearful of any mention

of this dimension. Many educators and administrators I encounter find it difficult to understand this difference between institutional religion and matters of the spirit. To ignore the spirit, though, and to attend only to the cognitive, emotional, and physical needs of young children is to risk the meaninglessness and emptiness that we see in so many young people today.

Since our public conversations about children ignore the ineffable and unexpected, we live in a time of spiritual crisis. In our society more wealth has been created for more people than in any society in history. Republicans and Democrats fight to take credit for this net increase. Yet no one will take responsibility for the spiritual emptiness and thirst that also pervades our culture. Personal and private despair lie in the wake of this period of unprecedented economic growth. Independent schools are composed of the most affluent families in America. Yet, most headmasters will tell you that people are less happy and angrier now than at any other time. Amid houses of treasure, fathers rage; mothers anxiously wring their hands and hover; children, ungrounded, float and fritter.

When our lives are so out of balance, the time is ripe for a spiritual revolution. So many have so much and wake up each morning still feeling an emptiness; they trudge off to work to get more stuff to fill up on and wake up the next morning, empty.

Our public vocabulary reflects the lack of meaning in our work. As a school head, the same words and phrases flow past me each day. These are the terms of the wealthy twenty-first-century American: happiness; value-added; branding initiative; success; managing growth; going to scale; product line; flexibility; customer service; learning styles; ADHD everywhere, in school and in the workplace; maximizing shareholder or stakeholder value; brain wiring; confidence; state-mandated testing; clients. The language of physical science and the terminology of business inform and dominate the work of social service agencies, churches, and schools.

And why should these groups not appropriate this vocabulary? The two most obvious, measurable, successful human endeavors in our culture are medicine and business. Those of us who work with children think that if we can only employ the concepts and techniques of science and business, our industry too will grow powerful and influential.

Still, we yearn for something more. Sociologists and psychologists have long studied people's motivations for becoming parents. Birth control is both available and reliable, and the economic and career benefits of not having children are evident in a postagricultural and postindustrial society. (Some economists have even argued that for some groups—for instance, privileged, well-educated women—it is just not rational to have children.) Still, we haven't witnessed any appreciable drop in the birthrate. And in the wake of wars and national tragedies like 9/11, the birthrate actually goes up. Even with articulate groups like Childfree Families, who strive to make it socially acceptable to choose not to have children, most people decide to have children or plan on doing so one day. Indeed, many women undergo years of torturous reproductive procedures in order to conceive. Why? Social science cannot with any kind of empirical precision explain the drive to conceive, except to say that many people are biologically driven to reproduce.

Here is one suggestion. We continue to have children because we are driven to love. Despite the predominance of instrumental rationality in our culture and an economy based on greed and self-interest as a means to lift all boats, we still yearn to give and to share. The other day, a friend of mine told me that investors are now seeking companies that make pet products. It seems that more people than ever own pets, and they indulge and pamper their dogs and cats with all kinds of goods and services. I interpret this as a sign of a basic human desire to love, nurture, and take care of a life.

We don't hear much about love today. In fact, I never hear the word used among educators. When we talk about parent education, we never say that what we're really talking about is love education. Certainly, a politician would be embarrassed if she said her goal was to make us a loving country. When George W. Bush, as a presidential candidate, said that the greatest philosopher of love, Jesus, was the thinker who most influenced him, I almost, for just one minute, thought that he would add love to the Republican Party's platform. Perhaps love makes us blush; academics are not taken seriously when they discuss love. It's considered a "soft" topic.

I can understand why business people and elected officials don't talk about love (though it would be so refreshing and liberating if they did). But why do people who work with children avoid the word? Why, when we talk to parents about raising children, do we shy away from discussing the dimensions of love? In English, love is a vague word that entails so many connotations that it is almost a meaningless term. Other languages recognize the varieties of love and give them different expressions. As mentioned before, in Greek, *eros* means physical love, *philos* means an intellectual, abstract appreciation, and *agape* means a spiritual connection. In my Italian dictionary, I count nine different words and phrases for love. Maybe we have such a hard time speaking of love because our language is not rich enough in this area.

Nevertheless, most parents will tell you that they experienced, for the first time, their capacity for unconditional love in the ineffable and seemingly miraculous connection they felt when their children were first born. Before having children, love may have meant companionship or sexual attraction and conquest or a mode of possessiveness. Love may have meant attachment to work or to an idea. In our youth, loves came and went; passionate flirtations flickered and faded. We may have felt loved by our mothers and fathers, but all too often this love seemed to us to be stultifying and smothering. Our parents' love seemed an emotion perhaps to keep close, but not too close.

As part of their love, parents may even develop a bit of religious faith in this moment. By faith, I do not mean a sensation of hope. I am speaking of faith in the way the Danish philosopher Søren Kierkegaard wrote of a "knight of faith." Kierkegaard's knight of faith is a person who expects the absurd to occur, even though the absurd cannot on logical and experiential grounds ever be expected to happen. Parents are knights of faith in that they expect the unexpected.

With our children, we somehow lock into another being. Unlike so many other relationships, this new relationship is for life. It involves a previously unimaginable physical intimacy. There are times when you will not sleep for two nights because of colic, and you realize that your daily anxiety and exhaustion are never going to end. Tonight they cough and wheeze, but soon enough they will date, and you'll still be up all night nervously waiting for their safe return. At one time or another, every parent understands with shocking clarity that children are not a four-year degree or boot camp. They are not a trial to be endured and mastered. Your child becomes the permanent framework of the rest of your life. They become your fixed compass point, your context for making meaning.

When my son was two, my wife and I left him with her parents and visited friends in a hunting lodge in Colorado. While they relaxed and communed with the mountains and the streams and the lovely meadows, we pined for seventy-two hours. We could only think of and talk about our son. We only wanted to get back to Buffalo and hold him in our arms. Not having learned our lesson, when our second son turned two we went away again. My wife and I spent the entire weekend quoting the two boys and, echoing the boys' favorite interest at the time, pointing out every construction vehicle to each other. "Look, Erme," I would

say, as we toured the Alpine wine country of the Finger Lakes
Region, "there's another backhoe!"

Parental love is a gravitational pull from which you will never
be released. It is a kind of haunting. We are caught in the grip of
our children. Parents who have lost their children often speak of
them in the present tense. When making small talk, one friend,
who lost her youngest of three in a car accident, always says that
she *has* three children and their names *are* Harry, Joyce, and Mike.
She told me she uses the present tense because she's in a kind of
denial. She knows her son has died. But he still exercises a pull on
her. He's still a palpable force in her life. He is present.

If parenting is about anything, it is about this kind of love. I do
not mean "about" in the sense of equivalence. I mean "about" in
the sense of puzzlement, proximity, and experimentation, as when
we say that a rock climber scurried about the face of a cliff. This
sense of "about" suggests immediacy, urgency, movement, testing,
failure and retrial, being alive and astir. "About" also implies a constant presence, as when we say that there are ghosts about.

When broken into its etymological parts, "about" literally
means "on by out." Parental love is being on and by and out of a
child. It is feeling the pain of the lost teddy, even though you
know you can just march down the street and buy the exact same
one. Like the knight of faith, parental love is absurd. Is this not a
mode of grace, then? We are given so much from seemingly out
of nowhere, and yet, this gift entails a great and urgent responsibility. Parental love is so profound because at its most elemental,
it teaches us to accept our children and ourselves. Acceptance and
love do not imply indulgence. Love is the tableau against which
our acts of discipline and prodding are performed.

In a recent *New York Times* interview, the novelist Richard
Russo explained that his unhappy characters are the ones who
lack "the wisdom to love the life they've been given." I can think
of no better way to characterize parental love. As parents, we have

been given a life, and from somewhere we get the strength, the courage, and the wisdom to love this life we have been given. This is a life that is utterly its own and yet is our responsibility forever. This is a life that is completely separate and individual and yet always a part of us. It is apart and a part, which is why we are so connected and so helpless.

Though we are helpless, we are not hapless. I know so many families who may not go to church or attend a synagogue but feel compelled at the end of each day to say a sort of prayer. Before bed or at dinner, these parents ask their children to tell them the best part of their day. I ask that our community of parental seekers, who wish to explore the greater depths of their love, reflect each day on their time with their children and ask the same ques-

∽

Parental love is a kind of haunting. We are caught in the grip of our children.

∽

tion. From the early morning sound of footsteps in the hallway leading to your bedroom to the clank of breakfast dishes to the brushing of teeth to the selection of clothes to the rush to the car to the grocery store aisles to the negotiations over television time versus chores versus homework to the gobbling down of dinner to a bee sting to the begging for an extended bedtime to bath and stories and finally to a groggy goodnight and the sudden slam into unconsciousness of an exhausted child's sleep: Ask yourself, as you nod off, what the best part of your day was with your child. In the midst of your anxiety and frustration, the question will force you to reconnect with the wisdom of happy people. It will, in the end, help you to give thanks.

Share this thanks with another parent, not as gossip, but as a form of fellowship. If we can forge a community of newborn bards of the holy parental spirit, perhaps, just perhaps, love will return to the public conversation. Love will be allowed to inform our institutions. Teachers and civic leaders can begin to talk about the place of love in education and policy. Parent education will become the equivalent of love education, rather than a system of checklists or reminders and techniques. Love will then, in Merton's words, define our depth of awareness within which the daily dramas and chores of parenting life will reveal themselves as hierophanies. . . . If only we had the space and the permission to look.

In a way, I wrote this book as a way to give myself this space and permission. It is a hard book to end, for it represents a journey that is far from finished. Each day, I witness yet another episode to include. I could have included so many more chapters. I have not considered the theological aspects of picky eaters, night terrors, doctor visits, pets, chores, clothes, cartoons, Internet Web sites, friendships, swimming, summer camps, food shopping, playgrounds, and school performances.

There is so much to see once we begin to look.

The End

Works Cited

Barfield, Own. *What Coleridge Thought*. Middletown, Conn.: Wesleyan University Press, 1971.

Bayard, Louis. "Was That Elijah?" *New York Times Book Review*, October 5, 2003, 18.

Blake, William. *Selected Poetry*. New York: Penguin Books, 1988.

Buber, Martin. *I and Thou*. New York: Charles Scribner's Sons, 1970.

Carlson, Ron. *A Kind of Flying*. New York: W. W. Norton, 2003.

Clausen, Christopher. "Childfree in Toyland." *The American Scholar* (Winter 2002): 111–21.

Dewey, John. *Democracy and Education*. New York: Free Press, 1944. Reprinted 1966.

Eliade, Mircea. *The Sacred and the Profane: The Nature of Religion*. New York: Harvest Books, 1968.

Emerson, Ralph Waldo. *Emerson in His Journals*. Edited by Joel Porte. Cambridge, Mass.: Harvard University Press, 1982.

———. *Essays and Lectures*. New York: Library of America, 1983.

The Fire Sermon. Translated by Bhikkhu Thanissaro. www.saigon.com/anson/ebud/ebsut026.htm

Fisher, Philip. *Wonder, the Rainbow and the Aesthetics of Rare Experiences*. Cambridge, Mass.: Harvard University Press, 1998.

Fremantle, Francesca, and Chögyam Trungpa, trans. *The Tibetan Book of the Dead*. Boston: Shambhala, 1975.

Fuchs, Nancy. *Our Share of Night, Our Share of Morning*. San Francisco: HarperSanFrancisco, 1996.

Gardner, John. *Nickel Mountain*. New York: Alfred A. Knopf, 1973.

Heidegger, Martin. *Being and Time*. New York: Harper & Row, 1962.

Hendra, Tony. *Father Joe: The Man Who Saved My Soul*. New York: Random House, 2004.

Holy Bible. New Revised Standard Version. New York: Oxford University Press, 1989.

Kant, Immanuel. *The Philosophy of Kant: Immanuel Kant's Moral and Political Writings*. Edited by Carl J. Friedrich. New York: Modern Library, 1949.

Kierkegaard, Søren. *Fear and Trembling*. Translated by Alastair Hannay. New York: Penguin Books, 1985. Reprinted 1988.

Lethem, Jonathan. *The Fortress of Solitude*. New York: Doubleday, 2003.

Mascaro, Juan. *The Upanishads*. New York: Penguin Books, 1965.

McGrath, Ben. "Vermont Postcard: The Light of Sunday." *New Yorker*, December 1, 2003, 38–39.

Matthews, Gareth B. *Dialogues with Children*. Cambridge, Mass.: Harvard University Press, 1984.

———. *The Philosophy of Childhood*. Cambridge, Mass.: Harvard University Press, 1994.

———. *Philosophy and the Young Child*. Cambridge, Mass.: Harvard University Press, 1980.

Merton, Thomas. *The Asian Journal of Thomas Merton*. New York: New Directions Publishing, 1975.

———. *New Seeds of Contemplation*. Boston: Shambhala, 2003.

Miller, Barbara Stoler, trans. *The Bhagavad-gita*. New York: Columbia University Press, 1986.

Milton, John. *Paradise Lost*. New York: Odyssey Press, 1962.

The New American Bible. New York: Benziger, 1970.

Nouwen, Henri J. M. *Life of the Beloved*. New York: Crossroad, 1992.

Nussbaum, Martha C. *Upheavals of Thought: The Intelligence of Emotions*. New York: Cambridge University Press, 2001.

Pickthall, Mohammed Marmaduke. *The Meaning of the Glorious Koran*. New York: New American Library.

Plato. *The Dialogues of Plato*. New York: Random House, 1920.

Pollack, William. *Real Boys*. New York: Random House, 1998.

The Revised English Bible. New York: Oxford University Press and Cambridge University Press, 1989.

Smith, Huston. *The World's Religions*. San Francisco: HarperSanFrancisco, 1958.

Shakespeare, William. *The Tempest*. New York: Penguin Books, 1970.

Stearns, Peter N. *Anxious Parents: A History of Modern Childrearing in America*. New York: New York University Press, 2004.

Thoreau, Henry David. *Walden*. Princeton, N.J.: Princeton University Press, 1973.

Trungpa, Chögyam. *Cutting through Spiritual Materialism*. Boston: Shambhala, 1973.

Waley, Arthur, trans. *The Way and Its Power: A Study of the Tao Tê Ching and Its Place in Chinese Thought*. New York: Grove Press, 1958. Reprinted 1980.

Watts, Alan. *Behold the Spirit: A Study in the Necessity of Mystical Religion*. New York: Vintage Books, 1947. Reprinted 1971.

Weber, Bruce. "Richard Russo: Happily at Home in Winesburg East," *New York Times*, July 2, 2004, B25.

Index

agape, 61–62, 148
Augustine, Saint, 80
awards, 100–110

Bayard, Louis, 9
bedtime stories, 84–86
Bhagavad-Gita, 2
birth, 13, 117
Blake, William, 36–37, 121
Boehme, Jakob, 72
Brooks, Albert, 40–41
Brooks, Mel, 128
Buber, Martin, 14, 31
Buddhism, 35, 43, 45, 62, 65,
   66, 70, 72–73, 91, 109
Bush, George W., 148

Carlson, Ron, 87
change, 118–19
Childfree Families, 147
Christianity, 64–65, 91
Coffin, William Sloane, 80
Coleridge, Samuel Taylor, 36, 38

college admissions, 106–10, 121
College Summit, 128–32
communion, 81–82
crucifixion, 44
curriculum development, 37

death, 119–21
Dewey, John, 108–9
disappointment, 25–31
discipline, 63–71
Dylan, Bob, 44, 145

Eckhart, Meister, 35
Eliade, Mircea, 12, 44
emergency rooms, 137
Emerson, Ralph Waldo, 38–41,
   98, 144, 145
emotions, 47–54
epistemology, 18–24, 114, 132
Erikson, Erik, 85

failure, 133–43
faith, 15, 145–46, 149–52

Fisher, Philip, 116
Frankenstein, 75–76
Fuchs, Nancy, 85

Gardner, John, 133
Gilligan, Carol, 121
gossip, 90–99
grace, 37
growth, 109–10

happiness, 122–23
Hebrew Bible, 2, 44, 64, 66
Heidegger, Martin, 91, 96–97
hell, 72–80
Hendra, Tony, 118
Heraclitus, 119
hierophany, 12–17, 44, 81, 152
Hinduism, 65
hobbies and interests, 100–110

idolatry, 109
imagination, theory of, 36–38
Immaculate Conception, 112
Islam, 63–64, 65, 91

Jesus Christ, 43, 44, 72, 78–79,
        97
Judaism, 64–65

Kant, Immanuel, 29–30, 138–40
Kaufmann, Walter, 14, 30
Kierkegaard, Søren, 149
knowledge, 10–12, 18–24

Lethem, Jonathan, 115
Lotus Sutra, 2
love, 61–62, 147–52

Matthews, Gareth B., 115–16

Mays, Willie, 105
Melville, Herman, 68
Merton, Thomas, 12, 54, 152
Milton, John, 72, 76, 77
mysticism, 53
Muhammad, 43

naturalism, 15
New Testament, 44, 66, 78–79
No Child Left Behind Act,
        124–25
Nouwen, Henri, 71
Nussbaum, Martha, 48–49, 55

parents and parenting
    abusive, 9
    aesthetic, 8
    dutiful, 7
    influences on children, 72–80
    motivation to become, 147–52
    narcissistic, 8
    pragmatic, 11
    religious, 8–9, 12–17
    rescue hero, 5–7
Picasso, Pablo, 36
Plato, 116
play, 32–38
    and mysticism, 35
Pollack, William, 52–53
Proust, Marcel, 85

questions, 111–21
Qur'an, 2, 64, 66, 72

rationality, 52–53, 76–77, 123
religion, definition of, 16, 93
revelation, 92–93
rituals, 81–89
Rolling Stones, The, 1, 39–40

Russo, Richard, 150
schools, 122–32

Schramm, J. B., 129
Schwartz, Delmore, 38
sin, 63–71
Socrates, 116, 177
soul, 126–27
standardized testing, 124–25
Stearns, Peter, 4–5
Steiner, Rudolf, 117
sublime, the, 138–41

Talmud, 97
Taoism, 35, 36, 65
Tao Tê Ching, 2, 14, 65
Telushkin, Rabbi Joseph, 97
Tempest, The, 121
therapy, 77

Thoreau, Henry David, 18, 23, 24
Tibetan Book of the Dead, The, 72–73
toys, 55–62
transitional objects, 55–56, 85
Trungpa, Chögyam, 66

Upanishads, 17, 65

Watts, Alan, 21–22
Wellesley College, 4
What to Expect When You Are Expecting, 2–3, 16
Wilde, Oscar, 53
Winnicott, D.W., 55
wonder, 116–17, 121, 132

Zen Buddhism, 8, 45, 46

About the Author

The Crossroad Publishing Company is honored to offer book readers the first book from a dynamic young author and educational leader, Dr. Keith Weller Frome. For many years, Dr. Frome has been active in finding innovative ways to teach young students and empower parents. This interest includes his formal academic training. Dr. Frome holds an EdD from the Teachers College of Columbia University, with a concentration on Religion and Education. His other degrees include the MTS (Harvard University Divinity School); MA in philosophy (University of Connecticut); and BA in philosophy (University of Hartford), *summa cum laude*.

Dr. Frome has also been an active teacher, in roles as diverse as adjunct associate professor, religious studies, Canisius College; writing coach coordinator for College Summit; preceptor in expository writing (Harvard University); and researcher (Lawrence Kohlberg's Bronx Project).

Dr. Frome's experience in publishing extends across his tenure as associate executive editor at Columbia University Press and his current role as contributing editor to the cutting-edge *Traffic East* magazine, where he has contributed essays on themes such as Thoreau, landscape and spirituality, and Zen. He is editor of *Hitch Your Wagon to a Star and Other Quotations from Ralph Waldo Emerson* and (with Richard Marius) *The Columbia Book of Civil War Poetry* (both from Columbia University Press).

A popular public speaker, Dr. Frome has addressed gatherings around the world, including The Oxford Round Table at Oxford University, College Summit National Training, the National Association of Independent Schools National Conference, The Book Forum in Manhattan, and the Philosophy of Education Society.

The editors at Crossroad remember one speech with special fondness—Dr. Frome's eloquent speech on "Provocation as Vocation: Emerson and the Ministry," delivered to faculty and students in the chapel at the Divinity Hall of Harvard University, April 14, 1988.

In a manner of speaking, from that day we have been waiting almost twenty years for Dr. Frome's book to come to fruition. We believe *What Not to Expect* has been worth the wait.

Dr. Frome currently serves as Headmaster at the Elmwood Franklin School in Buffalo, New York. He lives in Amherst, New York, with his wife and two sons.